Unleash
S.E.X.Y.

Experience Love, Happiness and Success Being Irresistibly You!

By

Mudrika de Maria
Entrepreneur / Speaker

"The sexiest thing a woman can wear is the confidence of being irresistibly herself!"
- Mudrika de Maria

Printed in the United Kingdom

First Printing: November 2020

ISBN: 978-1-936839-38-4

Dedication

YOU… my courageous reader …may you Unleash Your S.E.X.Y. and dance through life experiencing love, happiness and success being irresistibly you!

P.S. With a touch of sass and sophistication!

Acknowledgements

My delicious girls, Melania and Sienna, you inspire me every day with your unconditional love and zest for life.

My mum for teaching me to treat people with love and kindness.

Marcus, the father of my children and business partner, for pushing my buttons and helping me grow to be the best version of me. Above all, thank you for our best productions, Melania and Sienna. Thanks for your support in writing this book.

All the men in my life. You have been the epic mirrors… my catalyst for change… I thank you for showing me all my fears and insecurities. . . equally showing me love, respect and trust. My dad, for your values and strong work ethic. My brother, my rock! Thank you for your unconditional love.

All you S.E.X.Y. women in my life. You are the perfect box of chocolates... your support and love are second to none, and I couldn't have made it without you in my darkest hours. But above all, thank you for all the laughter, fun, joy, dancing, singing, nights out, holidays, shopping and pamper time.

My World Class Team for your support, encouragement, hard work and dedication to helping me live my purpose.

A special thank you to Ann McIndoo, my Author's Coach, who got this book out of my head and into my hands.

My amazing clients who remind me daily to Unleash my S.E.X.Y.

The Universe (God, Higher Self) for always delivering opportunities and gifts of life... throwing me on the epic rollercoaster of life.

FOREWORD

As a mom of three, business owner, international speaker, author, and entrepreneur, I know what it takes to succeed, whether at home, in relationships or in business. Mudrika has also figured it out: You can have success being a feminine woman and the very best version of yourself – at the same time.

That is what Mudrika experiences every day, the very best version of herself.

Mudrika has overcome a diverse set of challenges, both personal and professionally, and is a perfect example that anything is possible, if you want it. It's possible for everyone to be successful when one is committed. Mudrika has learned how to grow and develop her magnetic feminine energy and will show you how to create and develop your own. This book is about being irresistibly yourself and will teach you eye opening and simple ways to feel loved, happy and successful.

In Unleash your S.E.X.Y., Mudrika shares her life experiences, and has assembled the vast amount of knowledge she has learned and experienced as her identity, energy, and vision shifted in the various areas of her life, including wife, mother, investor, entrepreneur, and businesswoman.

With her sassy sense of humour, this story is filled with great strategies for being S.E.X.Y. in addition to being fun, light and relatable to all women – regardless of age, or race.

Mudrika has woven in her passion for beauty and fashion into this book and created a three stage journey: "Spa Detox", "Makeover" and "Runway Ready", which are a fun and feminine journey to reconnect to your S.E.X.Y.

Unleash Your S.E.X.Y is straight talking, down to earth, real and genuine. I look forward to keeping my copy of this book close by to teach, implement and remind me that I am S.E.X.Y., inside and out!

Loren Lahav
International Speaker / Author / STAY True CEO
"Life Tuneups" voted by People Magazine Most
Inspiring Book of 2010
www.LorenLahav.com

CONTENTS

Preface i

Introduction 1

Spa Detox Stage 5

Understand Why We Can't be S.E.X.Y. 7

What is S.E.X.Y. to You? 21

The Art of Letting Go of the Baggage 33

Makeover Stage 47

Reconnect to your S.E.X.Y. Self – Your Inner Magic 49

Connect to your Heart, Body, Soul and Intuition 59

Find Harmony by Balancing Your FeM Essence™ 75

Runway Ready Stage 87

Power Up Your S.E.X.Y. Self Inside and Glow Up 89

Slip into Your S.E.X.Y. Self Outside and Turn Heads 101

Catwalk Your S.E.X.Y. Self on the Runway of Life 111

Turn on the S.E.X.Y. WOW! 119

Preface

Thank you for choosing to read this book, it takes a great deal of courage to want to learn, grow and make a change in your life. I love the saying, *"when the student is ready, the teacher will appear."* This has always been my experience. For me, my teachers and mentors have been people who have put up mirrors in front of me to show me where I am holding on to old baggage that no longer serves me.

Today I am grateful to have the life I have where I feel S.E.X.Y. (Self-Confident, Empowered, Xtremely, You) and am experiencing life with, love, happiness and success. It has not always been this way and if I can do it – SO CAN YOU!

In the 1960s, my parents came to the U.K. with £5 in their pocket, to a country where they couldn't speak the language, to give my brother and I a better life. I am in awe of their courage.

With them came all they knew, which was our culture from home. I was brought up with a strong Hindu religion and a very strict upbringing – it was a very difficult time being a first-generation Indian to integrate into the western culture, going to school with different people and their own cultures.

I really didn't like school – I am a very creative person, and academic work just was not for me, however, coming from an Indian culture – this was everything! I got married at the age of twenty-two, as this is what is expected in our culture – the marriage didn't work out. I didn't know what I wanted from life at that age, let alone from a marriage.

My mum died six months before I was going to get married. I could have cancelled the wedding, but I didn't want to because she knew where it was going to be, and she would be there in spirit.

My first marriage did not work out as we were so young when we married, and we drifted apart as I looked to pursue a career and grow to be who I wanted to be. Sadly, we both decided to part ways after counselling and attending my first personal development seminar in June 2001.

After the personal development seminar, it was my dream to open a salon. I followed this dream which I did with lots of passion, resulting in having three salons in six months and did well financially. I was very proud of this accomplishment and loved my business.

By this time, I was married to my second husband (Marcus), who also was on a self-development journey. Together, we started a joint business, Investment Mastery. Investment Mastery's mission is to help our clients create financial independence for themselves and their families through financial education. Marcus is the Trainer/Speaker and face of the company, and I run the business as the Managing Director. This was a very exciting time as Investment Mastery was doing really well, so I gave up my salons and dream business to do what I believed was the right thing and work on the financial future we wanted and raise our family.

Marcus found working together as business partners great and supportive. It was not the same for me. I found working with my husband in a business very difficult. All we did was work and talk about business. It was hard for me to stay in my feminine energy, and over the years this started showing up in our relationship. We had children, which put more pressure on our relationship. At the same time, our business took an expansion internationally, with Marcus running workshops up to thirty weekends a year and away from home.

Running the businesses (we have a property business as well), running the home, bringing up the children on my own and Marcus being away meant I was juggling way more than I could handle. As the years went by, the more I struggled to keep my balance, the more I lost my S.E.X.Y.

This took a toll on our relationship, and we drifted apart. When we finally realised this was no longer a marriage, we worked with a relationship coach to see if we could re-spark our relationship, but we both decided it was best for our future to separate. Having worked on ourselves so much and mastered our communication skills over the years, we have the beautiful gift of still being friends and business partners.

My second divorce! I can't tell you how hard this was for me. I felt like a failure, that I'd let my children and family down, and that I was going to be judged by everyone. However, we both knew deep in our hearts and souls we deserved the lives we desired and settling or compromising was not an option.

Anything is possible if you believe and own your true self. Look at me today, sitting here writing a book! Before I unleashed my S.E.X.Y., I would never have believed I could write a book because I simply thought I was not educated enough and therefore not good enough.

Introduction

The book is not about being anything new, but who you always were, connecting to the incredible person you already are.

After becoming a mum, I faced a lot of challenges, the worst ever, really. Juggling my businesses, being a mum and a wife was overwhelming. I totally lost my sense of self. I really struggled and felt that they were some of the worst times of my life. I had such an abundance of resources around me and despite having done what felt like endless years of personal development, I still struggled.

Even though I had trained in several therapies, I was still not able to snap out of it myself. I hired a coach, but all the time was thinking, "Here we go again, can someone give me a break for a change? How much more help do I need?" When talking to my friends, I realised that they too had challenges just like me. Some of them spoke about it while others put up a front. I had thought it was only me and everyone else was happy … "the grass is always greener!" Suddenly I no longer felt alone. Working on myself, we went back to the real basics. After a year, I was back at 100%.

I may have lost myself when I became a mum, but now I had found a better me! As people saw the change in me, we started talking about it more. Over time I realised I had twenty years of experience, much of it trial and error, but also 20 years of learning, growing and knowledge from courses I had attended all over the world. What I now thought was normal or common sense was met with astonishment and gasps of admiration by those around me.

It is my philosophy, S.E.X.Y., that has kept me on track. I also feel I have had so many different experiences as a woman with an ethnic origin, lack of education, relationship break-ups, two divorces, miscarriages, weight gain, yoyo dieting, motherhood and running a business, that I can show others they are not alone. What took me twenty years of trial and error, they can learn in one book.

I can hold their hand and wrap my arms around them and show them the way to a better, S.E.X.Y. life. I wish I had discovered this all in one place. I could document all this information in one book. My two girls could always refer to it as they get older and see that anything is possible.

I wish to share my philosophy to help empower other women to be the best version of themselves, so they can do or be anything they desire. My purpose in life is to inspire and empower people to be the best version of themselves.

I've always had a vision, no matter how large or small, to make a difference, even if only to one life. This book is for women, and being a woman, I am writing it from my perspective. However, men will also benefit from the majority of the book with learnings they can take on too, including understanding the women in their lives. Ladies, if your men read this book, hide your mirrors!

Here are some of the main struggles women go through:

- Feeling unsexy, unhappy, unloved or unfulfilled.
- Losing themselves, their identity and their way
- Feeling stuck, overwhelmed and fearful.
- Aspiring to achieve more in their life but don't know how to move forward

Generations have changed, men and women's roles are no longer so easily defined. For example, when I grew up, my parents had clear separate responsibilities. Now with women working in careers and owning their own businesses, they have to do so much more. The world has changed, but we are not being taught how to cope or what to do about it.

So, how do we cope as a modern woman? We don't! We are losing who we are, our way, as we struggle with the overwhelming lack of balance. As you journey through life, different events will occur, and this may cause you to lose or need to evolve your identity. My hope for you is that this book will give you the teachings you need, to cope with your identity losses and shifts, throughout your life. These teachings will allow you to experience love, happiness and success, the feminine way.

You will learn to live a more whole life and in harmony with yourself, to know when you need to tap into your feminine and masculine energies, no matter what you are doing. We will also cover ways to tap into your intuition, for you to invoke this superpower. This book is a little "woo woo" and a little "do do."

WHAT IS S.E.X.Y.?

- ♦ Self-confident

- ♦ Empowered,

- ♦ Xtremely

- ♦ You

HOW TO USE THIS BOOK

I am talking from my own experience, take what you like, ignore the rest – this is your unique journey and experience. The philosophy I share is not about only learning new stuff, it's also about unlearning some of the crap that you may have picked up along the way, which really doesn't serve you.

Be open to a new way of thinking. You don't have to fully understand everything. It may get uncomfortable at times, trust the process, keep going. If you feel emotional … go through the emotions, write them down in the book, cry, scream, shout – let the emotions out! Change takes courage, I promise it will be game-changing…

Words are very powerful, and we all attach different meaning to words. I may say something that does not sit right with you, please change it to your own words. For example, I make reference to the Universe a lot in the book. For me, the Universe is everything as a whole, including God, spirit, divine power etc. Please replace it with what it may be for you.

One size does not fit all. Find your own unique ways. You will get to know yourself better so that you can live life with your rules and on your own terms.

S.E.X.Y. Share and S.E.X.Y. Social Shares

These are some simple tips and ideas that are scattered throughout the book – I call them a **S.E.X.Y. Share.** Use them and enjoy them. Then there is **S.E.X.Y. Social Shares**, where I encourage you to empower other women, by sharing your journey, stories and pictures on socials. Remember to tag me in, so I can cheer you on and celebrate with you! Let's support each other!

These are the main two:

Instagram: www.instagram.com/mudrikademaria

Facebook: www.facebook.com/groups/mudrikademaria

You can also follow me on YouTube:

YouTube: www.youtube.com/mudrikademaria

And you can contact me on my website:

Website: www.mudrikademaria.com

I have put together some free resources for you. You can find them at www.mudrikademaria.com/MClub

S.E.X.Y. Share

If it gets a little overwhelming, choose one thing and do it. Small steps also make a change! You've got this!

"You can be gorgeous at thirty, charming at 40 and irresistible for the rest of your life."

- Coco Chanel

Spa Detox Stage

CHAPTER ONE

UNDERSTAND WHY
WE CAN'T BE S.E.X.Y.

MEET THE UnS.E.X.Y. ME

Felt unloved, unhappy and unfulfilled

- Lost passion for life and my identity

- Experiencing life like I was spinning 100 plates 24/7, completely overwhelmed

- Comparing myself to others and feeling like a victim

- Self-loathing of my body, thought I was unfeminine, fat, and ugly

It was when I had my second child that I completely lost my confidence, I lost my S.E.X.Y. I didn't feel empowered and I didn't even know who I was anymore. I completely let myself go; I just couldn't be bothered. Self-care was a word that no longer existed in my life!

This was not my standard or who I am and despite knowing what I had to do to change it, I was just stuck. This was one of the lowest times in my life. There were times when I wanted to drive into something and end it all. I saw no light at the end of the tunnel. The only thing stopping me was that I would see my two little girls without a mummy, so I would put on a brave face and keep going.

In personal development, we are taught to master our emotions. But being a woman, this suppresses our natural need to experience emotions and release them. We need to cry. We need to be emotional. This can result in many problems, such as gaining weight. And boy did I do that – my love for pizza took on another level of obsession!

I used to be immaculate all the time, and now, I wore big T-shirts and leggings to cover up the weight I had gained and I wouldn't even shave my legs or shape my eyebrows. Mother Nature kind of took over my body.

I ordered clothes online and tried to connect to my love for fashion and beauty. I ordered things to make me feel good, lots of expensive retail therapy! Sound familiar? Yet nothing looked good on me, and instead of building my confidence, I felt worse, and I took on the famous, "I'll do it tomorrow" mindset. Damn, I was in a RUT!

Sometimes we are so busy playing different roles that we spiral out of control. We put ourselves on hold, and we lose our self-esteem and our self-confidence. It takes a wake-up call to think, "Okay, I really need to do something about this", but it can still go on for years and years before you realise something is not working for you enough to make the change.

My wake-up call was my eldest daughter hugging me one night and saying, "Mummy, what's that?" It was a roll of fat on my back just under my bra strap. I will never forget that day. I went to my room and cried, feeling I was letting them down. What kind of role model am I? What am I teaching them?

Running a business, with children was the hardest thing I have ever done in my life. No one teaches you how to deal with the transition to motherhood, let alone to be a mother AND run a business at the same time.

As time went on, I started getting myself together on the outside. My niece, a beauty therapist and make-up artist, started giving me treatments and pushing me to get my sh*t together – some new clothes and membership to Weight Watchers. So I started showing up well on the outside, but inside was not sorted at all.

Mastering your emotions, hiding your vulnerabilities and thinking positive is not easy. I showed up to work reasonably dressed and put on the classic front women put up. No one would ever have known at work what was going on behind the powerhouse entrepreneur, as I always showed up professional. Even on three hours of sleep when the girls were sick.

As the girls grew older, I started feeling a little more in control as they started becoming more independent, and I started working on what was going on inside. Today things are very different, but the battle was hard even though from the outside it looked like I had a perfect life.

THE EVOLVING WOMAN A.K.A. "SUPER WOMAN"

I believe the change amongst our generations, the higher divorce rates and break-ups, are because we are confused as to who is responsible for what, like raising the children or holding a career; men are confused, too. There hasn't been anything to teach or remind us of the value of maintaining this balance. And how do we maintain this balance, when we are all just winging it along the way doing the best we can?

Both men and women have feminine and masculine energy. When women get overwhelmed with trying to be a "superwoman", we can easily go into masculine energy which pushes us into our heads. Masculine energy gets our mindset on accomplishing one thing and pushes us away from being in our feminine energy. This is covered later in the book.

S.E.X.Y. Share
"I don't mind living in a man's world,
as long as I can be a woman in it." - Marilyn Monroe

Many times, women, for so many different reasons, get lost in who they are. They lose their S.E.X.Y. This applies especially to the evolving woman because women have such diverse roles. We wear so many hats, have so many responsibilities in life these days, such as wife, mum, sister, daughter, a career woman, holding up a few jobs, as well as taking care of the home. We get overwhelmed, lose balance and become resentful or unhappy. We feel the need to "go, go, go" all of the time while juggling all of these roles at once.

We often begin to feel unnoticed and unappreciated due to being overwhelmed by all our responsibilities especially when there is a stroke of bad luck such as the loss of a job, a loss of a family member, a break-up or divorce.

We lose connection to who we are, we go last on the list of priorities, and before we know it, we have lost our S.E.X.Y.

UNDERSTANDING HOW WOMEN TICK ... AND THE UnS.E.X.Y. 7™

In no particular order, below are The UnS.E.X.Y. 7™

1. Denying our Emotions
2. Over Giving and Depletion
3. I'm OK!
4. Disney Princess Syndrome – Lost Reality
5. Disease to Please
6. Need to be a Good Girl
7. Guilt

What is important is that we understand how *we* tick. Women are built a certain way - to love and nurture. Most of the time, we are not taught how we tick. We simply pick up and follow patterns in our childhood from previous generations and the media. Ask yourself, "Did I take that pattern on from something or someone else?" "Is it something my parents used to say or do a lot?" I still hear my mum in my head, saying, "Why are you doing that?" "You shouldn't be doing that." Is it a teacher who impacted you? A sibling? A significant other? We can catch the patterns we have learnt along the way to better understand where they came from. More about this is chapter three.

No one teaches us what patterns we should and shouldn't have taken on. So, to be the true you, you must look really deep to rediscover your authentic self.

1. DENYING OUR EMOTIONS

Women are emotional beings, and we should own that! To help us find our S.E.X.Y., it is absolutely ok to cry – it is our emotional release. We cry and get it out of our system, and all of a sudden, we feel a lot better. This doesn't mean going to the supermarket and crying every two minutes – it is about knowing it is ok to feel emotions and what triggers us.

Denying our emotions, learning to control them and staying positive for the sake of it can have a big toll on our body because our body is not meant to do that. Suppressing my emotions and being positive, resulted in me having a number of health challenges. I want you to know it's ok to be vulnerable, so feel your emotion, own it!

In today's world, we feel we have to be superwomen, and we are not allowed to be emotional in a man's world. Men will just think we are irrational and crazy. Crying in a boardroom may not be appropriate at times, but if needed, go and find a secret crying spot and let it all out.

Once we realise that we are emotional beings, we can then find ways to accept our emotional reactions and be able to say "ok! I am feeling this way, so how am I going to deal with it at this moment, and how can I support myself?" Men often go out and get active physically to let it all out. That is the way they deal with their emotions. Women may simply need some emotional support such as a talk or a hug, a walk in nature or a little cry to deal with theirs.

S.E.X.Y. Share
I have found over the years that simply talking to my friends about what's going on allows me to express my emotions and find solutions to my problems.
Having a supportive community is huge!

---

2. OVER GIVING AND DEPLETION

Women are natural givers. We are nurturers, we are built to look after the family, so it is biological. We feel it is our responsibility to give, give, give. It feeds the soul. If we don't find the balance, then we easily get ourselves depleted and don't always understand exactly why.

Sometimes, we may over give love to receive love from others; a woman with high feminine energy - her top desire is love, to give it and receive it.

When we don't give, it could make us feel guilty because we feel we should be giving more. It can spiral out of control, and we can get a distorted view about how much we should be giving. Women tend to put others first; it generally comes from watching our parents or others do this as we grow up. We see role models doing this, and we emulate their behaviour.

You must give to yourself first, then you can give freely to others; otherwise we feel depleted. Think about pouring water into a teacup sitting on a tea saucer. The water symbolises giving… as you fill-up the cup of water its starts spilling over and it catches in the saucer. Well, you are the cup; you fill yourself up first, so you are filled with everything you need, and then you give from the overspill in the saucer. Giving is absolutely fine, but we have to give from a place of excess.

3. "I'M OK!"

We are so good at pretending we are fine, aren't we? We only say that to stay strong because everyone else appears to be fine around us. I was guilty of doing this for years after I had my daughters. I remember running my business and doing the school drop off all suited up. I would see other women in their activewear. I'd think how great their lives probably were, being able to take care of their bodies and have coffee with their friends, whereas I was completely overwhelmed with having to get up early and get everything done before I left the house.

I always answered, when anyone asked, "I'm ok, I'm ok." I remember talking to these women later in life. They said they would have done anything to have had been in my position as an entrepreneur and seemingly, my life together, and able to take care of my family.

"I'm ok," when you are not is a load of crap! We must be real with our emotions and what we are feeling. The grass always appears greener on the other side. We all have stuff going on in our lives, it is just different stuff. Come on, hands up, who is guilty of saying this?

S.E.X.Y. Share

Even a strong person needs a hug and someone to tell them, "Everything will be alright."

---

4. DISNEY PRINCESS SYNDROME – LOST REALITY

There is something I refer to which is Disney princess syndrome. I love Disney, I am a huge fan and always have been, and the movies have evolved over the years, which is great. I am sure some of you will relate to the time when you were growing up with them.

Who else grew up with the idea of a prince who is going to come and save the day, we will fall in love and live in a castle, and all will be great? If we live in a world out of touch with reality, we will expect to be a princess with riches handed to us and a prince charming who is perfect.

We equally scroll through social media, forgetting it may have taken over ten pictures and hours of make-up, hair and fashion to have gotten that one perfect shot. Let alone the various angles taken or the filters added. Losing touch with reality and having fairytale expectations can push us into victim mode, sitting around, waiting, and not doing anything for ourselves.

The same applies to movies. I love movies, and what woman doesn't love a good rom-com? Again, here we can pick up the dream and not the reality of how life should be. We can use it for inspiration, but we also have to put in some of the effort. Yes, there is the power of visualisation and manifestation, which I do believe in, but even with that, some action is still needed.

5. Disease to Please

We have a disease to please, this again is picked up in childhood. If you are good, then you get love, affection and praise from parents or school, and I am very guilty of this, coming from an Indian culture.

I was taught to please all the time, to respect my elders; I had to be of service to them, and everyone in the community did the same. I realised that I took this into my life, into my career, friendships and marriages, I saw the pattern that I was pleasing because that's how I thought I would get love and recognition.

By over pleasing or pleasing with an expectation to receive something and we don't receive what we are expecting, we feel unappreciated and build up massive resentment.

6. Need to be a Good Girl

We are taught to be good girls via our parents, schools and figures of authority. We learned to be a good girl, say "Please", "Thank you" and "Sorry", do what everyone wants. As a result we would receive appreciation, recognition, praise and potentially love. My friend who is a Reiki healer heard me saying "Good girl" to my daughters. I had even made up a song with positive affirmations in it that I used to sing to my girls before bed and it has the words, "Good girl" in it. My friend told me to stop saying that.

I asked why and she said I am programming them to always be a 'good girl' for me, and not allowing them to be and express who <u>they</u> are. I thought, "Gosh, that was from my own childhood." I was moulding them to be copies of me and not themselves, so I stopped right away.

Are you being a 'good girl'?!

7. Guilt

Guilt is when we have conflict or think we have violated our beliefs or standards. These beliefs are likely to be strong patterns that have been picked up from your upbringing, thinking you have to act and be a certain way. Guilt can often make us feel like we should be punished because we have done something wrong when in reality this is not true. Due to the nature of our feminine needs, we tend to feel more guilt than men. It is important to question if the guilt we are feeling is ours or just patterns that have been passed to us, that no longer serves us.

You are not alone, I promise! So many women are going through the same thing in different ways. When I share these insights with other women, I find every single one had experienced not feeling S.E.X.Y. and some have had it harder than others. It took me twenty years of trial and error to unleash my S.E.X.Y. and maintain it and still to this day, I learn, grow and evolve, and still have patterns show up.

Don't settle for anything less – settling is not S.E.X.Y.!

TIME TO REFLECT

UnS.E.X.Y. 7™	Do any of these apply to you? On a Scale of 1-10 score yourself (1 = hell no, 10 = absolutely)
Denying your emotions	8
Over Giving & depletion	4
"I'm OK!"	9
Disney princess syndrome lost reality	3
Disease to Please	5
Need to be a Good Girl	7
Guilt	6

ANY "AHA" MOMENTS?

What did you just discover about yourself?

I need to break out of my masculine energy.

Chapter Two

What is S.E.X.Y. to You?

What is S.E.X.Y.?

S stands for **S**elf-confidence, E stands for **E**mpowered, X is **X**tremely, and Y is **Y**ou. It is my personal philosophy of how we can live the most Epic life, full of love, happiness and success on our own terms. When you are called, S.E.X.Y., that is certainly a confidence boost, yes, but being able to call <u>yourself</u> S.E.X.Y. is the ultimate form of self-empowerment because you are not dependent on anyone else to feel great.

- ◆ Self-confident
- ◆ Empowered,
- ◆ Xtremely
- ◆ You

UNLEASH YOUR S.E.X.Y.

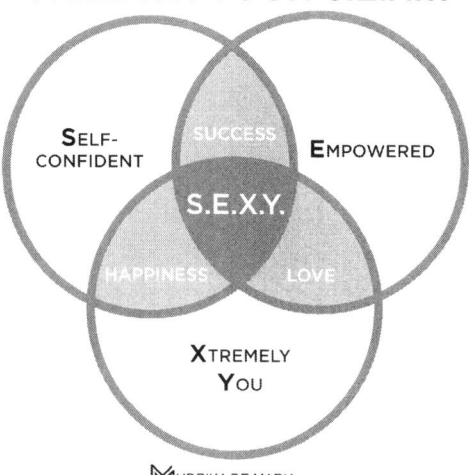

My journey of trial and error allowed me to come up with this proven method of transformation to, "Unleash your S.E.X.Y."

In my many years of working with women, in so many different ways, the most rewarding feeling is when THEY feel happy about themselves. They just glow and radiate! And become magnetic!

<u>Self-confidence</u> – is when you believe and trust in yourself, your strengths, abilities and character. You know your weaknesses and accept them, even embrace them. That's what makes you uniquely you. You have a positive view of yourself. You handle criticism well and not shy to voice your own opinion without worrying what other people think of you. You trust yourself.

<u>Empowered</u> – is having an inner belief and inner knowing that you have the power to affect your own life in the way you want. That you are safe and secure in the knowledge that you have the choice to control what happens in your life. Often people feel empowered by a belief in God or Universe or Mentor who transfers that feeling.

<u>Xtremely you</u> – is you fully expressing your personality with no fear of judgement. You love and respect yourself and live life how you want to live it regardless of people's opinions. You look to study and enhance what is already working for you, looking to improve on it so you can be the very best version of yourself.

You enjoy your passions and hobbies. They bring you joy and bliss. This raises your vibration. You can always see these people – they light up a room with their energy and vibe.

When you Unleash your S.E.X.Y. you feel like you have found a magic wand, life seems more real, easier and happier.

When I lost my S.E.X.Y., I found that I was not being my true self. I was used to being the crutch for everyone else or taking on everyone else's needs and challenges. I didn't even know who I was anymore! I knew what my passions were but was not feeling any of those either. I think being S.E.X.Y. is about totally owning who you are and loving that fully.

Most of the time, people don't even know what that is, and I feel like as soon as you find it, it is almost like finding a magic wand. The more you practice being who you truly are, the more empowered you become, the more self-confident you become. This allows you to totally Unleash Your S.E.X.Y.

The S.E.X.Y. 3™ areas of your life are:

1. S.E.X.Y. Self – How S.E.X.Y. you feel on your own - in your own skin

2. S.E.X.Y. Social – How S.E.X.Y. you feel when with others

3. S.E.X.Y. Sexual – How S.E.X.Y. you feel in your intimate relationships

We will mainly cover your S.E.X.Y. Self, as this is the foundation of all your S.E.X.Y. 3™ When you master your S.E.X.Y. Self, it will trickle into the S.E.X.Y. Social and Sexual. This is where you can be playful and spice up your life!

S.E.X.Y. Share
More S.E.X.Y. Social and Sexual tips in the M Club at
www.mudrikademaria.com/MClub

I know it sounds like a massive task right now, but as you go through this book, you will start having some realisations, maybe even some "Aha" moments, and that is enough to start you on your journey.

Many women find the word, sexy, intimidating. I am of course generalising here, but often we have a belief or an image of what sexy is supposed to look like.

In my opinion, being sexy is ok, but being S.E.X.Y. is the best way to being irresistibly you, it is sheer confidence. It is about totally owning who you are and living on your terms, being totally unique and authentically you. It is the freedom to express who you are. There is no comparison to others. There is no judgement of others or yourself. It is guilt-free, being in-tune with your feminine power. It is flowing and fluid. You are radiating your truest self, strutting your thing!

I believe this is truly the best way to experience love, happiness, and success. It is your God-given right to be who you were born to be!

THE WORD SEXY IS TABOO

The reactions I received about writing a book called Unleash Your S.E.X.Y. has been fun and interesting to see. I'm talking about S.E.X.Y. not about just sexual sexy. Sexual sexy is for the bedroom… or wherever you like.

We can sometimes see all sexy as bedroom sexy, due to the media and what our beliefs are about the word. I refer to S.E.X.Y. as our vibe, how we as women radiate and sparkle.

When they first saw the title, some people assume I'm having a midlife crisis. My answer to them was, "Nah, I've had half a dozen of those already … I'm a super achiever." The word is taboo, there are negative connotations to it, but for me, being a woman is being S.E.X.Y. and being S.E.X.Y. is being magical, mystical, sensual playful, and carefree.

S.E.X.Y. Share
S.E.X.Y. is the way you walk, talk and think.
Not your body.

Who is hiding the cover of this book, so no one can see what you are reading? Hold the book with confidence, enjoy the attraction it may bring. You may even start a conversation with a complete stranger and make new connections. Dare to be different... bring out the naughty girl inside! Take a picture! Put it up on socials and tag me in so I can celebrate with you!

SHIFTING YOUR PERSPECTIVE

Most women need a shift in their perspective. Being S.E.X.Y. is confidence and being your true you - it is not sleazy. I am not talking about going out just to flaunt your body and being fake or taking up pole dancing as a hobby. Side note: it is great for your core... and yes, guilty as charged! I have tried it and fell flat on the floor like a sack of potatoes! I am talking about the S.E.X.Y. that is becoming your truest essence, your true flow, and being exactly who you wish to be, not being worried about what others think or say.

You are not going to be someone else. Often, we look to copy other people who we think are sexy - a friend, work colleague, movie stars. When you take on other people's sexy, you may feel like you have to put on an act and pretend to be like them, which takes you even further away from who you are. When you are unsure of whether this is your S.E.X.Y. or not, it will not last for more than a short period of time. You will realise you are not happy or comfortable being this person, or that it just does not fit who you authentically are.

Are you being your S.E.X.Y. or someone else's sexy?

> ## S.E.X.Y. Share
> You are not too old to be S.E.X.Y. It is not too late.

INTIMIDATED BY OTHER WOMEN

A lot of women are intimidated by other women's confidence because they lack their own, as well as a connection to their true self. Any time you feel that intimidation, look at the other person and ask what makes you uncomfortable? What is it about this person? Is it that they are giggling out loud at a bar? Is it whether they are smiling or not? Are they getting a lot of attention?

Maybe you don't feel comfortable giggling that loud in public, or maybe you have been told in school or in other relationships to hush, to be quiet, to not draw so much attention to yourself. Maybe your parents taught you not to laugh loudly in restaurants, so you feel you shouldn't.

This is a great opportunity to reflect on what may be holding you back and help you get empowered!

USING WOMEN AS AN INSPIRATION

We can always use other S.E.X.Y. women as inspiration for us to find our own S.E.X.Y. My top favourites are Marilyn Monroe and Coco Chanel. They are so very different, yet inside, they are very similar in confidence, empowered and truly themselves. Wow, they were way before their time and inspire me even today.

They still had their successful careers and were still so S.E.X.Y. and feminine. I think that as time has gone by, technology has taken over and our brains have shifted. This has put us more into "doing" mode instead of paying attention to our intuition and feeling our feminine vibe.

Those two beautiful women were strong and successful but didn't have all of the technology bombarding them with new information and roles to play, with constant new goals to achieve. Successful women to me these days are more than just the successful entrepreneur; they are the successful mums, friends; they are confident and may not be outwardly expressing their S.E.X.Y., but they are still feminine and confident, which is beautiful.

I encourage you to admire women who are S.E.X.Y., not just the famous ones, but the ones in your everyday life; watch them and get curious, see what you think makes them S.E.X.Y. What can you take on and adopt? I say, why not!

BE YOUR OWN S.E.X.Y. THING!

In my opinion, every woman wants to be S.E.X.Y. Who doesn't want to think and hear, "You're so S.E.X.Y.?" It is the biggest compliment a woman can receive, just saying! I can see you nodding your head and that little smile, I saw that. *It is important to express yourself and to do your own thing!*

Do your own S.E.X.Y., not anyone else's. It has to be absolutely yours. You are not playing a role, and this isn't some kind of drama. We are not showing up on stage to act out our lives as to what we or society thinks sexy should be. It is about living it and expressing it as our own and on our own terms.

- Is it your own truth?
- Is it you?
- What are your dreams and desires?
- How do you want to show up in the world?
- How do you want to express that?

There are no rules for being S.E.X.Y. We think there are because of the modern world, the models, the filters and social media outlets that trick us into thinking everyone is perfect … and they are not.

We can put filters on us to look totally different. What happens is, we think if we are not tall and thin with shiny locks of curls and perfect lipstick, we are not S.E.X.Y. but only because we are comparing ourselves to others and their standards. This is about your version of you.

There are absolutely no rules. Most of the time, when we want to achieve anything in life, we think we are not good enough or worthy of living on our terms. Most of the time, we feel we need permission from the outside when, in reality, it needs to come from the inside.

We need to give ourselves permission to feel S.E.X.Y. and confident and beautiful. Living just as we are, not comparing ourselves to anyone else. S.E.X.Y. is about loving ourselves and having high self-worth, self-love, and knowing we deserve anything we want and having it all on our terms.

You don't judge yourself; you don't compare yourself to others, you are content with who you are. When you Unleash Your S.E.X.Y. you have a unique vibe about you, you become magnetic and draw people to you effortlessly.

S.E.X.Y. Share
Our body language is as powerful as our words;
it is how people perceive us.

FLAMBOYANTLY S.E.X.Y.

My favourite job was being a make-up artist for Christian Dior for six years. In this time, I grew to feel very S.E.X.Y. and confident. I loved what I did, and I was in my feminine flow. This was in my late twenties. I was young, glowing, free, and vibrant.

Now, at this beautiful age of forty-nine, it is a different kind of S.E.X.Y. for me. I do not necessarily want or need the same things now, as I did back then, to feel S.E.X.Y. Now, inner wisdom is S.E.X.Y. for me. It is more about sophistication and chic S.E.X.Y., which has evolved from what my idea of sexy once was.

We need to understand when, where and why we lost our S.E.X.Y. to get it back. Where are our challenges, where are they showing up? We must have a new way of thinking to solve this problem in our heads.

Let's get your S.E.X.Y. on! It's time to get out of your head and into your heart and body. When you are there, and you can truly be who you want to be, it is extremely freeing and a little flamboyant, and why not? Be yourself and don't compromise. You will only live once!

TIME TO REFLECT

- Is the word sexy taboo for you? No

- What does sexy mean to you as opposed to S.E.X.Y.?

- Do S.E.X.Y. women intimidate you? Why? No

- What S.E.X.Y. woman inspires you and why?

ANY "AHA" MOMENTS?

What did you just discover about yourself?

_____

_____

_____

_____

_____

For a printable exercise sheet for you to work through, go to

M Club at www.mudrikademaria.com/MClub

I'm excited for your progress!

Chapter Three

The Art of Letting Go of the Baggage

The Invisible Black Bin Bag on Our Shoulder!

Over time, we all gather up baggage full of patterns that do not serve us. I use the analogy of it being a black bin bag, because it's ugly, stinks and quite frankly belongs in the bin! When I am speaking at events or working with clients, I will get them to write on a piece of paper all the patterns they have picked up, all of their insecurities, scrunch it up and put it in a bin bag. Then, I get them to walk around the room with this bin bag on their shoulders and get them to walk past a mirror, to see how pretty it looks. I have to say it's not a great look! But it's a great way for people to visualise what they have been walking around with most of their life.

Whilst you are reading this book, whenever something comes up for you to bin, I want you to note it. I will have prompts for you at the end of each chapter but don't wait until then if something comes up sooner. Whether you write it down in this book, on a sheet of paper, in a journal or on a sticky note, write it down! Below I will explain what rituals you can do to let it go.

My plea to you with reading this book is that you will get rid of this ugly bin bag you are carrying around and replace it with a beautiful Chanel bag or whatever floats your boat!

LET IT GO!

"Let it go ... how do I do that?" I hear you ask. There are a number of exercises and rituals you can do. For this book, I will be using my bin bag exercise. If you find a way that works better for you, please use it, don't worry I won't be offended, I want what's best for you! Bring together all the things that have come up for you, from your black bin bag and do one of the following letting go rituals as often as you like, throughout the book. Here are a couple of variations for you to find what resonates with you:

- Rip the pieces of paper into tiny pieces or scrunch them up, feel that satisfying sensation and throw it in a bin

- Safely, burn the paper outside, reducing the patterns to ashes

- Bury the paper in the ground, send it back to mother nature and lay it to rest

My preferred ritual is to burn my paper outside on the ground and then mix the ashes into the earth. Some of your patterns may be quite deep-rooted, for these you may wish to get a professional to help you.

This exercise is a simple and easy way to let go and release what has been holding you back. When I do this exercise with my clients, they feel as if a great weight has been lifted off their shoulders. Don't forget to sling your new Chanel bag over your shoulder girls!

Understanding Your Unconscious Patterns and Insecurities

As mentioned, we pick up patterns as we go through life. Some patterns are good, and some hold us back, and you may experience this in different ways, like fear, or your inner voice telling you can't do something. Most of us run these patterns for years, some an entire lifetime because we are simply unaware, or Unconscious.

Where do the patterns come from? They are normally handed down to us from our family between birth and the age of seven. These are our most formative years, and this is when we spend the most amount of time with our parents, so we pick up the patterns from them. Now, of course, this is not their fault and they were doing the best they could at the time; however, these patterns may no longer be serving you. After all, generations have changed.

Did you go to a school where you wore a uniform and you were basically told to sit down, shut up, listen and repeat what you were told? This type of forced discipline taught us to be like everyone else and not to think outside of the box.

Do you have friends that get you down? Instead of helping you, they try to keep you where you are, not because they don't want you to be happy, but because of how it will make them feel and they will compare themselves to you. Other friends just don't want you to change because they like you the way you are and don't want to "lose you."

Media is the killer! If you believe you escaped the pro-gramming brought to you by your family, school and friends (and that's just not possible because you are just the sum total of everything you saw, heard and felt while you were growing up), then the media will finish you off. If you want to instantly feel sh*t about yourself, you need only a couple of minutes on social media to make you feel inadequate.

How you are raised in terms of religion, culture or life within your community can form many strong patterns of behaviour. My family cultural beliefs have had the biggest impact on my life. These cultural beliefs worked well in India but integrating them into the western world was a problem that no one was aware of. This is where most of my patterns that didn't serve me come from and has been the baggage I have been letting go of for the last few decades!

I always had a desire to be an entrepreneur, as I was inspired by watching my brother and dad running a business. However, I never believed that I was allowed to do that because I was a woman. I saw in my culture that men made the money, not women. In my culture women stayed at home and looked after the family, despite spending years studying for a career.

Another pattern that I took with me for years was that you must respect your elders without questioning. You don't ask, you just do it, and you are not supposed to have an opinion. Even when I asked questions about why do we do this or that,

I was told, "We don't know, the elders told us to do it so just follow it, don't ask questions, just get on with it."

How To Catch Your Patterns

Sometimes your patterns are not so visible. You have to look from the inside out and start reflecting on what is going on for yourself. You could choose to ignore them and feel like a victim, or you take action. When you are not aware, you are just walking around hypnotised by life. When you can see what is holding you back, you can embrace it as an exciting way to move forward. It is only when you are aware that something is holding you back, that you can begin to let it go.

Being aware of your patterns is the first step to change. I have found the easiest way to create awareness is to ask myself this question, "What is going on for me?" When I get triggered and someone pushes my buttons, I ask myself this question and start reflecting on why it made me uncomfortable. As mentioned earlier, people, especially loved ones, are often mirrors of what is going inside of us and they can push our buttons, trigger something inside of us that may need some attention or change. Such as "I am not good enough", "I am not loved enough" or "I am just so f**ked up."

Here are some powerful questions that you can ask yourself when you get triggered. "Why don't I like it here?" "Is it within my control or out of my control?" "What meaning am I attaching to this feeling and why?" These questions can be used in all areas of your life at work, at home, everywhere –

it has become a way of life for me. Most times, I work it through and where I don't, I will work through it with my mentor.

HEART AND HEADSPACE

These are two different places from which we operate. Heartspace is being in tune with your body and coming from a place of love which allows us to listen to our soul (our inner guidance).

Headspace is when we go into thinking mode, tending to overthink and over-complicate things, leading to feeling overwhelmed and shutting down our intuition. We start doubting ourselves, feeling out of control. The self-talk kicks in! When we over think things, there is normally a pattern we are running that can bring up fear and can often make up things that aren't even real!

Women tend to stack problems and make things bigger than they are; here is one problem, here is another and the next, and the next. Before you know it, we have twenty problems and even though ten of them are really small, we have been putting them all together and made a mountain out of a molehill. Nod your head if you relate!

When you are living in Headspace, you are pushing against the stream rather than flowing with it, making you feel depleted, and you can easily fall into victim mode. You start having self-doubt about whether you're good enough. You may start complaining, blaming people and situations, justifying things in your head, and it can make you over-emotional.

Because of this, you may start showing up negatively to others, needing external approval and hoping others will tell us we are good enough.

Living in your Heartspace is more natural and fulfilling, especially for women. This does require us to be aware of our negative patterns and triggers to be able to do that.

THE LINK BETWEEN HEADSPACE AND FEAR

Fear is important; it is our way of telling us there is danger ahead – KEEP SAFE! There are two types of fear: one is a rational fear, where your brain says, don't cross the motorway, don't jump off that cliff, don't touch the open fire, etc. The other is an irrational fear. Irrational fear is something that is made up in your head about what might happen. Most of the time, the fear is exaggerated and unreal.

So, how do we become fearful?

Let's say for example you're going on a night out and you decide to wear a sexy dress with a nice pair of heels. You put them on and look in the mirror. Fear kicks in, and you want to change to another outfit. What is that fear? Is it that you are going to be judged? Is it that people are going to talk about you? Is it that your shoes are going to hurt? These are irrational fears - one outfit isn't going to ruin your life!

Most of us pick up fear from our programmed patterns that we learn along the way in life. These are the things that we're going to be focusing on in this book to help you break out of, to help you break through and have more self-confidence. There is only one failure in life and that is not giving something a go!

S.E.X.Y. Share

Fear = F**K Everything And Run

OR

Fear = Face Everything And Rise

Below is a table to give you perspective on Heartspace versus Headspace:

Headspace (Fear)	Heartspace (Love)
Living in fear, feeling contracted	Living in love, feeling expansive
Living in the past or future fearfully	Present in the moment
Pushing and forcing life	Attracting life
Living in victim mode	Living in gratitude
Over analysing and complicating	Effortlessly flowing
Closed-minded and controlling	Open-minded and trusting
Disconnected and over-emotional	Connected and centred
Feeling overwhelmed	Having clarity
Tired and depleted	Flowing with lifeforce
BrainSTORMING!	Ideas just bubble up from inside

LOSS OF LOVE

When we are born most of us receive unconditional love, even if we look like an ugly lizard, everyone says, "Aww, how gorgeous and cute." We get so much praise for doing the littlest things, all the small milestones we reach. As we grow, we start exploring and things get harder for Mummy and Daddy, and we start hearing the no's, don't do that, don't touch that. We then go to school, sit down and do as we're told, we make mistakes and get told off. Suddenly, we feel inadequate and think getting love is conditional.

I remember at a very young age, I was such a daddy's girl. I've always called for him, hugged him, cuddled him, but the minute I hit puberty at the age of eleven, I was told by my mum to follow our culture, and out of respect for my dad, I was told to dress more appropriately. I was no longer allowed to hug him or sit on his lap. I didn't understand why I had to do this and what I had done wrong, so I started shutting down my emotions.

I felt I lost his love because I couldn't be tactile with him. Of course, I could be around him and I knew he loved me but being a very tactile person I felt like I couldn't get love from him. For many years I felt I didn't deserve unconditional love and that I had to please others to deserve their love, making it conditional.

NOT BEING GOOD ENOUGH

I felt I was not educated enough because I was constantly being compared to others in my community, and no matter how hard I tried, my academic results were never good enough. This stuck with me for many, many years. I just felt that I wasn't good enough because I wasn't educated enough, and I used that as an excuse for things that I wouldn't do. I felt I let my parents down, after all the work they did to move us to England, to give us a better education and a better life.

This led to me having a strong pattern that I was not good enough, and if I had kept that belief, I wouldn't be running my successful businesses now.

What patterns are you running?

SELF-IMAGE

When people took videos or pictures of me, I would blink all the time and drive my Social Media Manager mad. This triggered a memory of when I was younger. I was so uncomfortable having my picture taken because I had noticeable dark hair on my upper lip, and kids at school would tease me, saying, "I can see your moustache." This gave me a complex and when I was having a picture taken, I blinked my eyes, as I was self-conscious.

School is a commonplace to pick up self-image patterns, as kids can be mean, especially as they are trying to find themselves. Take a close look at those childhood memories.

TRAUMA

On one of our trips to India as a family, my mum complained of severe stomach cramps. She would wake up in pain and would say, "This stomach's going to take me to heaven." When we arrived back home, she got admitted to a hospital and they didn't know what it was. They put her into quarantine because she'd been abroad and about a week later, they diagnosed her with cancer.

Whilst having chemotherapy, it transpired that she was allergic to the treatment and she went into mass organ failure. She died on my 22nd birthday. I could not get my head around how my mother could die on the same day that she gave birth to me.

Within my culture, we believe in reincarnation and that a loss of a person is them passing onto a better life. I wanted to cry so badly at her funeral, but I was told not to cry or mourn as there was nothing lost. I held in my grief and my tears watching her lifeless body, seeing her for the last time. When I couldn't control myself and did sob, I was told to shush by several people. I was told that I would prevent her going to a higher place. I felt my temperature soar and did all I could not to pass out there and then.

The loss of a parent so suddenly – within weeks of being diagnosed – is one thing. Being told not to grieve is quite another. This experience was incredibly traumatic – I ended up shutting down my feelings and didn't release until 20 years later.

Twenty years of holding this in and not grieving impacted me massively, to the extent that I didn't think I could ever be emotional and in touch with my feelings. When we go through trauma of any kind, we must allow ourselves to process and accept the trauma, in a way that allows us to find peace. My release came as we started planning for my nephew's wedding. It brought back the emotions of my precious mother not attending my own wedding having died 6 months before I was due to marry. I cried before, during and after his wedding. No-one knew why but me.

We must find the courage within us to break free of the unconscious patterns that are holding us back. You may start feeling uncomfortable with things along this journey, but you will be able to understand why we embrace the changes that need to be made. It is an uncomfortable place, but the results are magical. I encourage you to get uncomfortable and reclaim who you are.

S.E.X.Y. Share
Everyone has their own sh*t going on.
It's just different sh*t.

TIME TO REFLECT

- Where are you currently living?

Headspace (Fear)	On a Scale of 1-10 score yourself (1 being low/10 being high)		Heartspace (Love)
Living in fear, feeling contracted			Living in love, feeling expansive
Living in the past or future fearfully			Present in the moment
Pushing and forcing life			Attracting life
Living in victim mode			Living in gratitude
Over analysing and complicating			Effortlessly Flowing
Closed-minded and controlling			Open-minded and trusting
Disconnected and over-emotional			Connected and centred
Feeling overwhelmed			Having clarity
Tired and depleted			Flowing with lifeforce
BrainSTORMING!			Ideas just bubble up from inside

- Any patterns or insecurities holding you back?

- What experiences and stories are you telling yourself?

- What's holding you back from the things you want?

- What fears do you have?

For example, "not good enough" "can't afford it" "not smart enough" "not confident enough"

- What triggers you?

ANY "AHA" MOMENTS?

Anything to bin and let go of?

_____

_____

_____

_____

_____

For a printable exercise sheet for you to work through, go to

M Club at www.mudrikademaria.com/MClub

I'm excited for your progress!

MAKEOVER STAGE

Chapter Four

Reconnect to your S.E.X.Y. Self – Your Inner Magic

Being Your True Self

Growing up, there was always an underlying feeling of not being able to express who I truly was. I used to be called a 'coconut' i.e. brown on the outside, white on the inside. I really wanted to fit into other communities and be friends with other cultures because I found it interesting.

People often used to tell me I was different. "You don't like fitting in, do you? You just have to always do things a bit differently, don't you?" "You can't wear a normal Indian outfit; you have to go with something really wild and mix up a Western and Eastern outfit together to do your own thing." I would receive many comments like these.

It was always important to me to have a personality, my own character, but within the community we were taught to all be the same. I always felt I was crying out to be the real me, and I think that was the hardest battle that I fought in those early years, even up until the age of thirty.

The Power of Being You

Being you is the most powerful thing you own; it is the deepest part of you. It is the magic of being the true you, the person you always were and are, it's not about being anything new. We are all born with our true self inside of us, and we are all born successful.

I refer to it as LIVING IN MY POWER! Living life on my terms, my rules, the ability to speak my truth and be my S.E.X.Y. self. I don't mean having power over others. I mean, who are you? How do you show up? Your authenticity is your true self. I struggled with knowing who my true self was after having children and I was in a fog. I hired a coach to snap me out of it, to wake up from my robot mode, stop living unconsciously. I couldn't even answer who I was, what my identity was or my self-image. I used to be an entrepreneur. Suddenly I was a mum, but also an entrepreneur. Which is more important? I am both, but what is my identity? Who am I, why do I feel so unhappy and disconnected? It was because I lost sight of my true self.

Years ago, I took a course and had to write down what my purpose was. Figuring out my purpose and who I truly wanted to be was an identity shift inside of me. It had always been in me but was told what I could and couldn't do. Being a pleaser, I did things to make others happy. I was just overloaded with other things, other people's beliefs and ideas along the way. Life happened to me, and I lost my way.

So, how do we reconnect?

We need to start by looking at what we loved to do when we were younger and compare it to where we are today. A lot of people don't sit down and look at this. We want to make changes but look for simple answers on the outside. Often, when working with clients, they sometimes want me to wave a magic wand and make things change for them.

Ultimately, the best place to come from is who you really are deep down. You have all the power that you need within you already. Looking for external sources is always difficult to maintain. It is time for you to really sit down and reflect on who you are. Most of us look externally for validation, but you have the ability to feel loved, happy and successful by yourself. Know you are enough and worthy!

S.E.X.Y. Share

Spend time alone, it is the fastest and most liberating way to learn about yourself. Oftentimes, we fill our time up being around people because it makes us feel better.

Reconnecting to yourself is a feeling, not a thinking thing. What makes you happy? What brings you into a place of bliss? This comes from within, it kind of just bubbles up rather than having to think about what it is or what it is going to be for you. We go through life learning, picking up patterns, as mentioned previously. We start believing life should be a certain way, we pick up other people's beliefs and start living up to other people's expectations of us: new skills, jobs, life experiences.

We get hurt, we fail, we have setbacks. This makes us put up layers of protection around us and start living life on auto-pilot until something happens that gives us some kind of wake-up call.

We often feel as though we need to fit in with the masses and do what others around us are doing. We do this to feel like we fit into a community, to be a part of a tribe. But when you are slightly different and embracing your unique skills, you are avoiding steamrolling over who you really are. You are not conforming. By conforming, we are forgetting who we truly are.

Let go of those layers and other people's shitty patterns. Time to say thank you but NO thank you!

When I had my wake-up call, I remember going back and starting to understand what was important to me at an early age. I discovered that the patterns, other people's beliefs and expectations of me that I had taken on weren't actually mine.

- Some may have been to please others and did not serve me well, however, they were still my decisions. It was only me who had taken other's beliefs on and not been confident enough to stand my ground or live my truth and say NO!

- Understanding this allowed me to take ownership, gave me the freedom to know I have the choice and has led me to live a more joyful life.

GOING BACK TO THE LITTLE GIRL INSIDE – RECONNECTING TO YOUR SOUL

I remember when I was a child that I loved to play with dolls and act as if I was a glamorous air hostess. Air hostesses in the 70s were very glamourous, sophisticated and feminine. When I look back I believe it was because I love to travel and be of service to people; it gave me a sense of adventure, new experiences, freedom, glamour, helping people – a sense of wanting to be free.

I also loved to dance. When I was about nine years old, I asked my parents if I could learn ballet. Coming from a strict Indian culture, they asked what the hell I wanted to do ballet for. They said no, we don't do that, we do academics, which is traditional for our Indian culture. However, they allowed me to do classical Indian dancing.

Later I wanted to sing and act, however, again, this was not regarded as what we do. But your soul, the true you, always knows and kept knocking for my attention and it was up to me to connect the dots. Last year I started salsa classes. I love it! My soul was craving it since the age of nine and it has always told me it is something I wanted to do.

What did you love to do as a child? What could you do for hours, where time just disappeared? There is a big chance that you still love those things, do you still do them? Your soul at a young age knew what made you that unique you, take a trip down memory lane to help you reconnect.

CONFIDENCE IN KNOWING AND APPRECIATING WHO YOU ARE

It is important to know that the things that you love, you love for a reason because they come from your soul. Although, you may have friends and family who have had varied interests and you got involved. What's important is to not spend all your time and energy doing what other people want to do, in order to belong. It's important to have the courage, to be true to yourself and do the things you love to do.

Tapping into and owning those things you love to do, those things that fill you up and light your fire will give you the capacity to be the bigger person in any situation. You are not competing. Everyone can be who they are, and there is no judgement, particularly of yourself. Getting to the point of being able to say, "That's just the way I am," is something to celebrate, and totally liberating!

There was a time in my life where I just wasn't listening to myself. Our soul always tries to knock on the door to remind us, to send us people that remind us of who we truly are and what we should be doing. I remember being at a seminar and a friend and I were making a poster of our goals. I remember her saying, "I really see you on stage, I see you empowering women to look great, to be great and feel amazing."

Deep down, I had always wanted to inspire and empower people, but I heard myself saying, "Shut -up. Me on stage, no way, I do beauty and make-up, how do I do that on stage!"

My friend replied, "Just put it down as your goal, or at least something similar." I could just about see the vision of it. Even though it seemed so far away, I did put it down. Interestingly, the soul always knows what it wants to do. Somehow it had to knock me around a good few times until I listen, and that was twenty years ago, and I'm writing this book today. There are no coincidences in life!

OWNING YOU

We need to recognise and take ownership of what may not have gone the way we wanted, that all the choices we have made over the years, we made for a reason. The reality is, some of those decisions caused us to take on a lot at any one time. From that, we may have looked to others for help or support and were sometimes disappointed with the response.

Sometimes we have to learn the hard way that we cannot look to rely on others to make us happy and feel good about ourselves. It is an inside job; no one else will focus on you (they are all dealing with their own sh*t). Make sure you are looking after you and are in a good place. Don't expect anyone else to dig you out.

LIVING IN YOUR CORE JOY/BLISS

Focus on those things you value: the things that you lose yourself in, where you literally warp time. Spend most of your time on the things you love.

Our soul always knows. Even back as a child, we may have been drawn to things for a reason – because it's who we are, it is who we have always been.

I was not allowed to dance, sing or act, but here I am today, sharing a message in a different way, via a book, social media, or on stage wanting to share my magic in some way. It is what my soul has wanted me to do all along. You, too, can take the journey from who you are today, back to the woman you were always meant to be, and move forward to live as a true, S.E.X.Y., wonderful woman from now on.

MUMMY GUILT

Even though I had help, there were a lot of beliefs around me being a good mum and being there for my children, that gave me quite a lot of mummy guilt. I remember speaking to a couple mummy friends and one said something that really stuck. She struggled having what she called 'mummy guilt', whether she worked or didn't.

She questioned herself, be a stay-at-home mum, or not be a stay-at-home mum? One of the things she said to me was what gave her peace was asking herself, "What role model do I want to be to my daughter?" I think that resonated with me because, even though I thought I wanted to be a stay-at-home mum, I really didn't enjoy being a stay-at-home mum. It didn't make me happy or fill me up. Spending time with them did but being a stay-at-home mum didn't.

I wanted to be a role model of being happy and being true to myself, doing all the things I love. Even though I felt at the time I had to be a stay-at-home mum, with our business, Investment Mastery, needing me I couldn't be. Needing to work was the biggest blessing on Earth. I didn't think it was then because I was being asked to choose not to spend time with my girls because work needed me. Ultimately, working and being a mum is what brought me joy. I share this story to show the importance of owning who you truly are, being able to make that decision from your core and that the Universe sometimes sends you curveballs to help. Knowing what works for you and what doesn't leads to a happy and fulfilled life.

TIME TO REFLECT

- What do you like most about yourself?
- What have you done that you're proud of?
- What did you enjoy doing as a child?
- What did you give up?
- What do you value most in life?
- What brings you joy and happiness?

ANY "AHA" MOMENTS?

Anything to bin and let go of?

_____

_____

_____

_____

_____

For a printable exercise sheet for you to work through, go to

M Club at www.mudrikademaria.com/MClub

I'm excited for your progress!

CHAPTER FIVE

CONNECT TO YOUR HEART, BODY, SOUL AND INTUITION

I was brought up with very strong religious values as a Hindu. My parents came to the U.K. in the sixties with a very small community. I used to really struggle with the teachings because I didn't understand the purpose behind it all. What is interesting for me is, although I don't follow the Hindu rituals, I have realised that in the new age spiritual teachings in the Western world, practices are very similar. Despite fighting my Hindu religion at a younger age, I now practice and appreciate certain teachings.

For example, Hindu culture teaches meditation, fasting, visualisation, gratitude, yoga, all of which connect you to your inner self. The term "being spiritual" really resonates with me, what about you? I believe being spiritual is getting out of your head and into your heart, body, soul and "owning your power."

S.E.X.Y. Share

Just a reminder, I personally use the term Universe and soul, feel free to use other words that resonate with you.

THE UNIVERSE HAS OUR BACK

The Universe is a connection to our higher self. It's the spirit that grows in everything, in humans, animals, plants or matter. The Universe is simply everything that exists. Everything that expands and grows individually carries its spirit. The Universe always has our back. It may not give us what we want, but it will give us what we need.

I have had misfortune, but the Universe always delivered in the end. My biggest lesson from the Universe was when I was trying to have my daughter. We tried for four years. I had the expectation of getting pregnant immediately, but that is not what the Universe allowed. I became pregnant and miscarried. This made me lose faith in the Universe because I thought I lived by the laws of the Universe, visualising, practising gratitude, treating people with kindness, no matter what.

I just couldn't understand.

The Universe had a different plan for me and waited until the right time to give me my first daughter, and when I was ready, my second. I find the Universe always makes things work, even when we are presented with obstacles, things always work out for our greater good.

The Universe nudges us and corrects our course to keep us in line with our true purpose. This allows us to stay connected with our true self.

THE S.E.X.Y. 6™ – THE POWER OF OUR SENSES

The most effective way for us to connect to the Universe is to use the power of our senses. Let me take you back to when you were a child. Think about how in tune you were with your senses; smelling flowers, licking an ice lolly, cuddling your toys, curiously looking to discover new things, remember how you were free as a child, easily distracted, moving from one thing to another.

As human beings, we have a number of senses. As we become adults, we go about using these totally unconsciously, not knowing that we've even got them. We start neglecting the power of our senses, as we live more in our Headspace, which does not serve us, especially for women.

We have five senses, in no particular order:

1. Smell
2. Sight
3. Touch
4. Hearing
5. Taste

When you connect to your senses, it allows you to connect to your heart, body and soul. First of all, we need to give ourselves permission to do so. To use our senses, we need to get out of our Headspace and into our Heartspace. A lot of women will say they don't have time for that but start with two minutes a day, then three, then four and so on, to nurture yourself.

SMELL

The sense of smell is totally underestimated and taken for granted. Smell has the power to change our mood and can trigger strong emotions. Being closely connected to taste, it can bring back memories from the smell of baking in your childhood or the person who had body odour and sat next to you at school. It can make you feel calmer, sexier and happier. Who doesn't love the smell of brewed coffee, fresh cakes baking or perfume that reminds you of someone you care about?

What/who do you love to smell?

SIGHT

Sight is the sense we use to explore what is around us. We use it to do nearly everything in our daily life, working, reading, driving, admiring a loved one. There is so much beauty to see around us, but we miss it with our blinkers on, such as trees, flowers, the stars and the sky. Have a little think about what you enjoy looking at and being surrounded by.

TOUCH

This is what we feel physically when we touch something or when something is touching us. Our skin is covered with millions of sensory cells, making it one of our most influential senses. This can be stimulated by different textures and touch, such as hugs or pets showing us affection. In my opinion, touch is a basic need, maybe not like hunger but without it, we can feel alone and out of touch with our feelings. What touch brings you pleasure? Is it something you wear? Is it having a shower or a massage? Is it hugging that fluffy cushion?

HEARING

We are surrounded by sound. We rarely have pure silence, there always seems to be some background noise in our lives. Often, we will be hearing but not listening to the sounds that bring us bliss, such as birds chirping in the background or leaves swirling along the ground. Music is one of the things that can lift and lower our mood instantly. You can create uplifting playlists that will make you want to dance like no one is watching!

TASTE

Taste helps us explore our world and different cultures, in the form of food. It helps us connect physically and emotionally to ourselves and others. When we go out for dinner with friends, it is as much about socialising as it is about the food. Taste allows us to connect to our emotions and we even call some foods comfort foods. Women will tend to get their emotional fix from food, more than men, because of our need to acknowledge and feel connected to our emotions.

6TH SENSE INTUITION

However, there is also a 6th Sense, which is often overlooked. *Intuition is your 6th sense.* Often, we don't realise the connection between the five senses and our intuition. Let me emphasise this again - Intuition is your 6th sense! Why am I repeating this? Because often we think of our 6th sense as being just another sense, but when you use several (3 or more) of your 5 senses, this magically activates your 6th Sense, intuition.

You know how people say, "I felt it in my heart, gut or bones" – do you ever hear someone say, "I feel it in my head"? No! Of course not. There's a clue right there. Get out of your head and get in touch with your senses and this will activate your intuition/feelings. At the height of intuition/feeling, you flow effortlessly in tune with your heart, body and soul. When you are in touch with your intuition, everything flows and becomes effortless.

Women talk about their intuition regularly but not many of us truly know how to tap into it anymore, and we totally under-utilise it.

S.E.X.Y. Share

Intuition is your god-given gift, it's your super-power.
Activate it! Use it! Own it! How?
"Get out of your head and drop into your heart!"

As kids, we would have used all of our senses and easily flowed in our intuition. It's no coincidence that as children, we may or may not have liked certain people without any logical reasons, it's likely we picked up on their vibe. As we grow older and go to school, we are told to sit down, shut up, concentrate, don't talk, and we start getting pushed into our Headspace. We are not taught how to stay connected to our intuition, and it is not acknowledged to be a skill. Sometimes we need to stop and nurture our intuition, slow down, and pay attention to our senses rather than our busy minds.

Listening to our intuition needs to become a ritual, something we do naturally. The more we listen to our intuition, the more we will trust it. At times, our negative little voice may rear its ugly head and will want to trip us up…tell it to "*F**k off kindly!*"

When we are connected to our intuition, we can use it in all areas of our life, especially where we think we can't. Let's take the example of our careers. Women tend not to use intuittion here. We think our careers must be done in a man's way because it has been a man's world, dominated by masculine energy. So, we come from a Headspace, as opposed to using our intuition to make decisions daily or when hiring, to sense whether this person is right for us to work with or not.

Sensuality shouldn't be mistaken for sexuality, even though you can use your senses in your intimate relationships. We must give ourselves full permission to enjoy our senses, without the connotations of it being sexual or doing it for someone else. Including, if you want to wear that silk nightdress and a splash of perfume to bed, to get in touch with your senses, do so freely! I can tell you I do this regularly and it makes me feel amazingly feminine.

WHY IT'S IMPORTANT FOR WOMEN TO LIVE IN THEIR BODY

Back in the day, we used to live in tribes. Before, women would be playing the specific roles, often together and be supporting each other. Whereas now, the roles are more varied, and our careers can lead us to be surrounded by men more, so we tend to get into our Headspace to communicate with them and end up staying in that space.

In a world of technology, we are bombarded by apps and social media, leading us to become overwhelmed and over-connected. Everything is so fast-paced, we are constantly in "go, go, go" mode. It is an epidemic. We take on new information thinking this could be the holy grail that will solve all our problems, but in fact – the holy grail is knowing who you are and being connected to your heart, body, soul and intuition. This will allow us to be in "flow" energy.

We can't change the modern world, but we need to evolve with it. We spend so much time sitting in a chair, working at a desk, driving from one place to the other. This is not good for our root chakra, which is our grounding energy located in our feminine womb area, as it means we are sitting on it blocking it all day. It is really important for women to keep connected to our senses and move our bodies, to allow the feminine energy to flow.

So what movement is key for us women? As my salsa teacher says, "Our hips, they don't lie." It is really important to move our hips. Get dancing and hula hooping, as even the little movements in your hips make a difference. A standing desk can be a game-changer because it gives you the freedom to move. I often swing my hips side to side whilst on a conference call.

S.E.X.Y. Share

Wear heels because they help to give you a sexy wiggle.

There's a reason Mother Nature is called Mother Nature and not father nature. We connect more naturally to her because she is the creator of life, as are we. Being in nature really grounds us women and similar to movement, allows us to get back into our heart, body, soul and intuition. For me, walking in nature is a form of meditation (mindfulness) as it allows me to be in the now.

THE S.E.X.Y. 5 TRIGGERS™

There are five unique triggers to unleash your senses. Normally we are triggered by things around us, often outside of our control. The S.E.X.Y. 5 Triggers™ come from you, and you control them to ignite your senses. They are simple yet powerful tools to use when you are in your Headspace and want to drop into your Heartspace. I've created five different categories, listed below, one for each sense.

TRIGGER 1 - S.E.X.Y. SCENT

Your signature scent is your favourite fragrance. It's your personal scent that you're either known for or what triggers you to feel good about yourself. It could be a perfume, an aromatherapy oil blend, a scented candle, or a bath bomb. Anything that really touches you lifts your spirit and connects you back to your senses.

I love perfume. I have a selection of my favourites for different occasions, and I love to wear them all the time, as it makes me feel S.E.X.Y., sensual, and noticed. I even leave the linger of my perfume behind, where often my team will say "I thought you were in as I smelled you, but I didn't see you."

S.E.X.Y. Share
"Make me a fragrance that smells like love."
Christian Dior

TRIGGER 2 - S.E.X.Y. LOOK

Your signature look is your style and empowers you when you see your reflection. It's how you choose to show up, how you dress and how it makes you feel. This could also include how you have your hair, accessories and make-up. It's an expression of you inside out and may be even a reminder of your personality.

I absolutely love high heels; they are the pedestal for my life. I love the way they make me feel S.E.X.Y. So does a fresh blow-dry, ridiculously long lashes and a chic blazer.

TRIGGER 3 - S.E.X.Y. THING

This is an item that you can touch and see that makes you feel empowered. It's something you attach meaning to that invokes a positive emotion. It can be a symbol, a logo, or it can be something physical like a picture, a book, an ornament. It is pretty much anything that you desire, the sky is the limit.

The meaning of my name Mudrika, in my religion, means ring. I've always loved rings and my S.E.X.Y. Thing is a Citrine stone ring, which is obnoxiously big. When I feel uneasy, especially in a business situation, I naturally play with the stone and it helps me get grounded again. You can have something in your pocket, where you reach in and touch it and it instantly gives you the emotion, e.g. Courage, you need.

TRIGGER 4 - S.E.X.Y. SONG

This is a piece of music that totally lifts you. When you hear it, it can make you wild and free or happy, excited etc. totally unleashing your S.E.X.Y.

There can be multiple pieces of music, depending on what mood you want to invoke. My absolute favourite, which you may have already guessed, is the song Hips Don't Lie, by, Shakira. It's just very feminine, sexy and makes me move my hips. I love the sexophone, oops I mean the saxophone and I'll have it in the background if I'm wanting to feel romantic.

TRIGGER 5 - S.E.X.Y. SECRET

This could invoke several senses and can stay totally secret, just for you. This is something you don't worry about because no one can see it unless you choose to let them. It could be a tattoo, a piercing, body jewelry or lingerie. It may not even be a secret; it might be something that you want to show on the outside. It's totally up to you. This one's more just for you and should make you feel cheeky and a little bit naughty.

My go-to has always been sexy underwear, for me it is the epitome of feeling S.E.X.Y. and confident.

S.E.X.Y. Share
I am 99% angel, but oh that 1% …

These S.E.X.Y. 5 Triggers™ have completely transformed my life and are my go-to when I am not feeling great. I would like to encourage you to explore your sensuality and use them as much as you possibly can in your daily life to stay connected to the beautiful, sensual woman that you are! It's who you are, it's what you stand for, it's like your signature – it's unique to you.

There is a template, on the M Club for you to print so that you can put it up on your mirror/wall to remind you. (www.mudrikademaria.com/MClub).

WHY DO WE LOVE THE SPA?

Most of us don't realise this, it is just something we women love to do. It's a treat, it allows us to pamper ourselves but when you look at it in detail, it is the perfect environment to experience all our senses being activated. You can smell the chosen calming blend of essential oils, lights dimmed, see some pretty flowers in a vase, listen to serene, tranquil music playing in the background, sometimes the sounds of a water feature and taste the choice of cucumber water or a herbal tea.

Then you get handed the fluffiest robe and look forward to a well-earned treatment. It is a great place to relax, let go and not worry about "go, go, go" mode and allows us to disconnect from Headspace and that busy modern world. As much as we all love going to the spa, you can bring the spa to your home by using your S.E.X.Y. 5 Triggers™.

THE POWER OF VISUALISATION/MANIFESTATION

Visualisation and manifestation are very similar, if not the same thing to me. I am a firm believer in the power of visualising, however I think sometimes it is taught in a way that makes us believe that we don't need to take action. I believe the Universe delivers your visualisation by putting opportunities in your path, for you to take action on. Sometimes these show up in the form of coincidences. What is important is that we are aware and open to seeing these gifts from the Universe, grab them and make your dreams come true.

Here is the best-kept secret to visualisation: do not visualise from your Headspace, because then the Universe can't hear you. The Universe hears you when you visualise with feelings. You feel the most when you connect to your senses because this connects you to your heart, body and soul.

So if you want to visualise, start with your feelings. For example, think of a loved one or your children, and feel the love you have for them. Then, from this feeling, move to what you want to visualise. The emotion will amplify your visualisation and attract it faster into your life.

TIME TO REFLECT

- How can you connect to your heart, body and soul more?

- How can you use your intuition more?

- What will be your S.E.X.Y. scent?

- What will be your S.E.X.Y. look?

- What will be your S.E.X.Y. thing?

- What will be your S.E.X.Y. song(s)?

- What will be your S.E.X.Y. secret?

ANY "AHA" MOMENTS?

Anything to bin and let go of?

_____

_____

_____

_____

_____

For a printable exercise sheet for you to work through, go to

M Club at www.mudrikademaria.com/MClub

I'm excited for your progress!

CHAPTER SIX

FIND HARMONY BY BALANCING YOUR FEM ESSENCE™

Yin and yang are a great analogy of two polar opposite energies, coming together to create harmony. Some examples of this are good and bad, light and dark, Heartspace and Headspace, love and fear. The one that I am most passionate about and seems to be the least taught is feminine and masculine energy.

FEMININE AND MASCULINE ENERGY

When I talk about feminine and masculine energy, I'm not talking gender, but about the specific energies that come from our nature. We all possess feminine and masculine energy, whether we are a man or a woman. We generally tend to have a core energy. A man tends to be more masculine at his core, and a woman tends to be more feminine at her core. The secret is to find the balance between the two energies and create your own individual harmony.

Each gender can possess each energy. A woman can have a lot of masculine energy, and a man can have a lot of feminine energy, and that's absolutely fine. A man can be in tune with his feminine energy and be nurturing with his children or be loving and understanding, as can a woman be in tune with her masculine energy in her career.

Both energies are needed to carry out different activities in our lives, but we can easily get unbalanced because we are unaware that we have moved away from our core energy and that's where we start losing ourselves.

Unbalance can show up in women, especially the evolving women who are juggling a number of roles because they get very much into doing energy. Doing energy is masculine energy that requires you to go into your Headspace. When in this space, it can create overwhelm, overburden and unhappiness.

Not being in balance will impact your relationships, specifically your intimate relationships, which I cover a little more in detail later.

S.E.X.Y. Share
If you're a woman with masculine energy,
and you're happy, then that's absolutely fine.
This is about finding your balance.

Below is a table to show how totally opposite the energies are.

Feminine Energy	Masculine Energy
Has a fluid energy and lives in flow	Has a firm energy lives in one mode, focused
Wants to experience love	Wants to experience freedom
Moved by emotions	Driven by direction and mission in life
Wants to fill up with love and attention	Wants to be empty and let go of his thoughts and burdens of life
Wants to feel understood and heard	Wants to be appreciated
Wants to be owned and desired	Wants to break free and have freedom
Looks to makes small thing big	Looks to make big things small
Wants to be noticed and praised	Wants to be challenged and win
Remembers and looks to hang on and fill up	Looks to let go, forget and empty
Fears losing love	Fears failure

Where are you living? Which is your natural flow? What is your natural energy?

When in feminine energy, we are fully present and grounded to mother nature, being vivacious, fluid, wild, free, full of life energy and connected to our intuition. The primary drive of feminine energy is to nurture. We are influenced greatly by our feelings and being open to love and giving love. When in feminine energy, we are in a continuous state of flow, looking for love to magnify our radiance and beauty. We become magnetic to others by opening our heart to beauty and love to fill up with positive vibes and attention. Therefore there is a desire to be seen as attractive, to be noticed and to be understood. This need is fulfilled by receiving praise and living in a sensual world, connecting to our body and soul. Some of the challenges that we face are that we do not find it easy to let go and can live in an overly emotional state.

In masculine energy, you have a strong physical presence, strength and centeredness. You are driven primarily by an unwavering purpose or direction in life. When in masculine energy you can only be in one mode at a time, and you search for problems to fix, even when one doesn't exist, as it is all about "go, go, go" energy. You have the need to liberate yourself from life and escape to ultimate ecstasy and freedom. There is a desire to thrive from a challenge, a need for competition, a want to possess and a need to feel appreciated. Some of the challenges faced in this energy are that it is too easy to let go, leave and speak from your head, lacking emotion.

THE CAREER WOMAN

I may have reached an abundance of success, but unfortunately, it was to the detriment of my feminine energy. I have always believed women should be financially independent because it gives us the freedom to do and have whatever we desire without having to rely on others. Which is why I have my own career and businesses.

I started my wealth journey in my feminine energy as I was working in fashion and beauty. But when I started my current businesses, my property portfolio and Investment Mastery, what I slowly started doing, without realising, was losing my feminine essence and energy. I looked very feminine on the outside, but inside, I was totally in my Headspace. I was being incredibly organised and efficient, and I was absolutely in what I call the "go, go, go" mode.

I was pretty much heavily into my masculine energy which is so out of my natural flow, which made me unhappy and overwhelmed. I found it extremely exhausting. In later years, I found out that I had adrenal fatigue because I was so in my masculine mode and against my core energy.

What is really important is that, even if sometimes we have to stay in masculine energy, we remember it's part of the game; it's part of having a career, it's part of having a business, and is part of creating wealth for ourselves. We do have to be in our masculine energy.

However, we have to also equally find a way to find the balance, and this is where I went wrong. I never knew how to find the balance. Having that masculine energy to push forward with our careers, being a wife and a parent can take over our bodies, not just our minds. We are always on the go and wondering what the next thing is, and the next, and so on.

During this journey, no one had taught me how to balance my energies or the importance of keeping that balance between your feminine and masculine energy. Especially for women who are driving careers and businesses because if you are in masculine mode but you're more of a feminine woman, it's very difficult to sustain this level of "go, go, go" mode.

PERSONAL DEVELOPMENT PUSHED ME INTO MASCULINE ENERGY

Through all the personal development that I have done over the last twenty odd years, the majority of it, almost all of it, was taught by men. They teach it from their space, not from a feminine space and, how would they? It is a lot of drive, force, and masculine energy.

What I discovered looking back was that this took me out of balance at the time. It was not until the last few years that I made this distinction and realised why I operated from such a masculine space in my life, which did not serve me.

Nowadays, there are a lot more feminine energy women teaching in this space, including growth, self-care and self-love. Which is great for us gals, but I still see a lot of women who are teaching from masculine energy. It is because we don't often know how to shift between the two. If you delve too deep into personal development it can be too much at times, especially when you receive different methodologies and strategies from different seminars. So make sure you are keeping true to yourself and in your feminine balance.

UNDERSTANDING YOUR FeM ESSENCE™

When you live in your feminine energy, you unleash the inner Goddess. Not everyone likes the word, Goddess, some use bossbabe – call it whatever you like. I like to call it the FeM Essence™, it is the perfect balance between our feminine and masculine energy and is a unique balance to you, it is your own internal Yin and Yang.

Everyone's balance of how they can operate in masculine or feminine energy is different, so we just have to find the middle-ground for you, so you can stay in harmony and in balance with it. This is also looking and seeing if you are living in Heart or Headspace. If you are happy with who you are, then it is likely you already are aligned to your FeM Essence™.

It is really about some trial and error, looking at what patterns hold you back! Reconnecting to who you are! Using your S.E.X.Y. 6™ Senses! This is where you need to use tools such as journaling and some homeplay I give you in chapter 9. Look and analyse where you are in "go, go, go" energy and where you are in "flow, flow" energy and see if you find a happy balance between the two. Personally, I do my best to live 70% in feminine energy and 30% masculine energy. This is when I am working in my business and where I must be in Headspace. This is my FeM Essence™ 70/30.

I look forward to you discovering yours!

COMMON CHALLENGES WITHIN INTIMATE RELATIONSHIPS

Sorry to get gender-specific here but I am going to share my relationship experiences and learnings. Most of the time men are coming from masculine energy and they don't understand feminine energy emotions. You will often hear them say, "she is just being a woman." It's true, men really are from Mars, and women are from Venus!

It is easier for a man to see problems as black and white. They look to solve the problem and will want to fix you or the problem. Whereas in feminine energy, we want to feel the emotions, be understood and often talk it do death.

Most women need attention to reinforce that they are loved and are important. As men generally are set in one mode thinking, things get lost in translation. For example, when we disturb a man who is watching TV and ask him a question, it confuses him as you have taken him out of his one mode. For the woman, it can appear that he is annoyed at her, that he is not interested in giving her attention and love, and that the TV is more important to him than her. Where actually, he is just trying to shift from one mode to another and appears confused and we think he is annoyed; but he isn't. That is just how masculine energy works.

A common trait amongst women is that they look to change their men to be more like them. We think that he may not be exactly how we want him, but he will change over time for me. It is not necessarily a conscious thing that we do, because we wouldn't want to change somebody that we love, nor would we want to date a version of ourselves. Remember, opposites attract.

It is interesting to pay attention to all of the differences between men and women. Men look at themselves in the mirror, and women look for themselves in the mirror. A man will think, "yeah, look at that haircut, I look hot" whereas a woman will look at themselves and notice what they think is wrong with them. Generally, women do this from a critical point of view. It is really important to break this pattern and compliment yourself.

S.E.X.Y. Share

Look in a mirror and say, "Damn, you're hot"
with a big S.E.X.Y. smile on your face.

The evolving times have led to both men and women not having specific gender roles anymore. Sometimes we can be out of balance and this can end up leading to the loss of polarity and attraction. It is good to be aware of this so that you can get into your core energy. When a woman owns her FeM Essence™ and is being herself completely, that is the most attractive thing to a man because she is magnetic; it's what we call chemistry, this is opposites attracting one another. You will turn heads, and it is the epitome of being S.E.X.Y.

One of the biggest lessons for me is that women need to be heard, understood and sometimes ramble on about a problem for hours, which is hard for men because it goes against their natural masculine energy. One thing I found helpful was to find more time to be around my girlfriends.

> ### S.E.X.Y. Social Share
> Pay your S.E.X.Y. forward by telling a friend
> that they are special. Don't forget to tag me in
> so I can celebrate with you.

GIRLIE TIME – THE IMPORTANCE OF BEING AROUND OTHER WOMEN

Spending time with your girlfriends and giggling, talking rubbish, drinking gin and crying is one of the best ways to get in touch with your feminine energy. When I had kids, I didn't do this as much and I got out of the habit.

I have met some amazing women who are my dearest friends, and we make jokes about finally having time to ourselves once the kids are dropped off at school or when we finished work. It was what we needed to bring the feminine balance back and not having to be everything to everyone.

> ### S.E.X.Y. Share
> When life throws you lemons, they say make lemonade!
> I say slice them up, grab a friend and make a gin & tonic!

When you live in your FeM Essence™, you are more in tune with your heart, body, soul and intuition. You are happier and will find achieving success to be more sustainable. Before, I would pick things up and never finish them because it was just too much "go, go, go" energy. Even finishing this book is a big deal to me because I am a real starter of projects. I go heavily toward something and it kind of fizzles out because I run out of "go, go, go" energy. Doing things in FeM Essence™ however, allows me to be in my "flow, flow" energy which is effortless. We can absolutely have success, doing it in a feminine way!

TIME TO REFLECT

- What do you think is your core energy, feminine or masculine?

- How often do you live in this energy?

- When do you most feel feminine, in "flow, flow" energy?

- What pushes you into your masculine or "go, go, go" energy?

- Do you have an idea of what your FeM Essence™ is?

ANY "AHA" MOMENTS?

Anything to bin and let go of?

_____

_____

_____

_____

_____

For a printable exercise sheet for you to work through, go to

M Club at www.mudrikademaria.com/MClub

I'm excited for your progress!

Runway Ready Stage

CHAPTER SEVEN

POWER UP YOUR S.E.X.Y. SELF INSIDE AND GLOW UP

You have now learned to understand the UnS.E.X.Y. 7™, let go of the baggage, be the true you, tap into your S.E.X.Y. 6™ Senses and you have found your FeM Essence™. It is now time to power up your S.E.X.Y. Self. When you work on your S.E.X.Y. Self inside, your S.E.X.Y. Self will automatically just glow up beautifully on the outside.

To power up your S.E.X.Y. Self inside, we are going to cover self-confidence and empowerment. What we need to do is understand what self-confidence is for you. What makes you your S.E.X.Y. Self? It's different for everybody. Self-confidence and empowerment go hand-in-hand. When you're feeling self-confident, you naturally get more empowered and when you're feeling empowered, you feel more confident. We will also explore how to fill up our emotional bank account, with self-love and self-worth.

S.E.X.Y. Share
The most epic love affair you can have is with yourself.

SELF-CONFIDENCE AND EMPOWERMENT

Self-confidence is knowing who you are, loving yourself unconditionally and having a high level of self-worth. How do you see yourself? What is your image of yourself? This could be known as your identity. Sometimes you can lose your identity due to a significant emotional event or some bad news in your life. The great news is you will have learned some skills, in this book, to reconnect back to yourself.

Self-empowerment is knowing you have everything you already need within you. It's about having choices. It's a feeling a sense of strength and power, it's positivity, hope, a place to learn and grow from.

It is really important that we respect ourselves. Oftentimes, we beat ourselves up. And that inner voice says, "I'm not good enough. It was my fault. I did that." Ladies, it's not always about beating ourselves up. It's about forgiving ourselves and being kind to ourselves. Everybody makes mistakes. As long as we learn from our mistakes and we grow from them, it's a beautiful lesson to learn. It is important to appreciate what you have achieved and done well in your life. This is true empowerment.

SELF-LOVE

I am excited to introduce you to our emotional bank account, which is my metaphor for how we measure how much we are living in our S.E.X.Y. Self. Are we overflowing in positive emotions, or are we depleted? Are we feeling good about ourselves, or are we feeling crap about ourselves?

Self-love is one of the main currencies to fill up our emotional bank account. Self-love is loving yourself first. We pick up patterns from various places, which makes us believe that we have to put others first, and this leads to us believing self-love is selfish. This is BS (utter BullSh*t!). Self-love is putting yourself first so that you can come from a position of strength and so have the ability to love others unconditionally and even help them.

Self-love is different for all of us because we're unique. I might feel self-love in a certain way, but you might feel self-love in a different way. We must give ourselves permission to love ourselves, in our own unique way, with the things that fill us up and give us bliss. When you get onto an aeroplane, they always say put your oxygen mask on first. They say that because once you have taken care of yourself, you can take care of all the other people around you. Now, if you went to put all those masks on your family first, you won't have any oxygen for yourself to live and you would end up not being able to help any of them.

If we can give ourselves love first and fill up our emotional bank account, we can give so much more because we are fulfilled and have no expectations of others. To have love for yourself, you must have the confidence to say no to the things that you don't want to do. This doesn't mean you're being a bad person. It's just about being true to yourself and living life on your terms.

Say, "NO!" more often!

S.E.X.Y. Share

Give yourself some self-love put your arms around yourself and give yourself a HUG. Be your own BFF.

I used to put all my family and work first. I had no time left for myself. I would put myself right at the bottom of the list, I wouldn't exercise or do things that filled me up. This is when I felt totally depleted and lost my S.E.X.Y. We lose ourselves over years of neglecting self-care. This is sad because self-care powers up our self-love.

It is important to keep your promises to yourself. This is showing yourself self-love, as you are continuously making yourself a priority. So, go book that thing that you have been promising yourself you will do. Why - because every time you don't do something for yourself, that you said you were going to do, you build patterns of not being a priority and your inner voice kicks in to beat you up.

00S.E.X.Y.™ (PRONOUNCED DOUBLE-O SEXY, LIKE JAMES BOND)

This is your ultimate self-care ritual. I just wrote above about giving yourself love. 00S.E.X.Y.™ is committing to that one thing, that is simple and easy to do on a daily basis, such as:

- Dancing for one minute, every morning, to your S.E.X.Y. Song

- Having one mindful meal a day

- Doing a two-minute stretch, to centre yourself and connect to your body

- Creaming your body, with the following affirmation "I love myself…I love myself"

- Having a cuppa in the garden

- Spraying that perfume that lifts you up

- Etc…

00S.E.X.Y.™ is not optional, it is a MUST to Unleash Your S.E.X.Y.

SELF-WORTH

Self-worth is about accepting yourself fully and knowing you are worthy of everything. We live in a world where a lot of expectations are put on us. We grow up with our parents and society saying that we need to get good grades, get into a good university, climb the corporate ladder, get a promotion and the list goes on and on and on.

There is always an expectation for us to strive for the next goal. For example, when you're single, people will ask you when you are going to find yourself a boyfriend? Once you have one, when are you moving in together? Once you live together, when are you getting engaged? When are you getting married? When are you having kids? And hold on, get this, this is just one area of your life! We end up thinking that life is always about achieving the next thing, and we don't feel grateful for what we have achieved.

And because these expectations weren't enough pressure, we now have at the click of a button, access to personal development and social media, telling us we must improve ourselves, and we must be a perfect size zero. This can leave us feeling unworthy and not good enough. Do you feel worthy? Do you feel good enough? If no, this is a great time to reflect and recognise these patterns, maybe revisit some of the previous chapters.

It's important to know that you are worthy of anything that you desire. A way to start feeling more worthy is to look at all the things you are good at and the things you are proud of. Start doing things that you love to do, things that fill your emotional bank account. It's about doing you, your 00S.E.X.Y.™ and talking to yourself with empowering language that reminds you that you are absolutely enough and perfect the way you are!

WHY DO COMPLIMENTS MAKE US SQUIRM

Women are the worst culprits of not accepting a compliment. You give a woman a compliment, she throws it right back at you. Women are their own worst critics, and therefore we find it hard receiving compliments. We feel like we have to justify why we look good. Who has heard this before:

"I love that outfit on you."

Reply "Oh, I've had it in my wardrobe for ages, it's only a little cheapo."

"I love that lipstick colour on you."

Reply "Oh, really, don't you think it makes me look washed out?"

How good are you at accepting compliments? Do you make excuses, or do you have enough self-love and self-worth to say, "Oh, why thank you?"

S.E.X.Y. Social Share

Share a picture of you giving yourself a compliment.
Tag me in so I can celebrate with you

JUDGE NO MORE

Have you ever found yourself judging a complete stranger, judging what they are saying, doing or wearing? Without even realising that you are doing it? People are a reflection of what is going on for us inside. Most of the time, judging shows up our insecurities and patterns. Do you know somebody that pushes your buttons? What is it that is irritating you about them? It is very likely that it is something that you don't like about yourself, something they may have that you might want to have or achieve.

I have on occasion, had feedback that people find me unapproachable. On talking to them further, this opinion generally changes because they realise that it's actually their own insecurities showing up. When I would ask what made me unapproachable, they would say I looked like a power-house, because I was well dressed and confident. As the conversations progressed, we found out that their insecurities were about their self-worth and self-image.

The worst judgement of all is the judgement of ourselves. So many times, I have seen people judge themselves, put themselves down, and it is one of the worst things you can do for your self-esteem. Judging ourselves is similar to comparing ourselves to others. When you do this, you are saying you are not good enough. If you are comparing yourself to somebody to be inspired by them, this is okay.

EXPECTATIONS ARE THE KILLERS OF SELF-LOVE

I was taught a lot of great values when I was growing up and learned a lot of great strategies on being organised and disciplined. With this, whether in my personal or working life, I would have unrealistic expectations and wonder why people didn't do things the way I did them. This would frustrate me and make me angry.

We tend to have a lot of expectations in our relationships, especially our intimate relationships. Which is the absolute worst! This is because of patterns that we have accumulated over the years or potentially what other people have done to us. We can often have expectations that are really important to us but are not important to our partner. Where not communicated this can create tension, resentment, arguments and ultimately end a relationship.

When you have expectations, and people don't live up to them, it makes you feel that you are not good enough or not loved. Often it's just not their way of showing up. Expectations will hurt you, more than they will affect the other person because they are likely to not even be aware of them.

For instance, if you send somebody a text, do you expect them to respond in a specific timeframe? And if they don't, how does that make you feel?

S.E.X.Y. Share

Love yourself so much that when you tell someone "I love you", you don't need to hear it back.

VULNERABILITY IS OK *AND* LIBERATING

Vulnerability is something that we fear because we think we're going to look weak, be frowned upon or be judged. So, we choose not to be vulnerable, we bottle it all up and keep it inside. It's a way of hiding our insecurities, our flaws. But that is a part of who we are; insecurities are a part of us, and it's when we embrace them and take ownership of them, then we can work on them. Every single person has problems. The only person who doesn't have a problem is one who is in a coffin!

Everyone is going through their own sh*t, but when we learn to be vulnerable, it really does set us free because it allows us to express and feel those feelings so we don't get trapped by them. I was very bad at being vulnerable. Having done loads of personal development and thinking positive, I used to bottle up all my fears and hide them from others.

I've learned by really being truthful and saying to the people in my life, "I'm having a really bad time, I'm struggling," has allowed me to feel much more supported. Sometimes we want to be the givers and helpers because this allows us to love, nurture and fill up our emotional bank account. So why not allow others to have the same chance to fill up their emotional bank accounts if they want to. Being vulnerable is living in your FeM Essence™.

S.E.X.Y. Share
There is nothing bad about falling apart.
Cookies crumble and fall apart,
but they are still loved by everyone.

DON'T BE A CONTROL FREAK

The evolving woman has to juggle a lot of roles and this pushes them into Headspace. We feel the need to control and project plan everything, because this gives us certainty, to ensure everything goes right as that is easier for us. Requiring everything to be done our way with no flexibility is exhausting, creates stress, and we become overwhelmed. Then we feel we have failed when it doesn't go our way and start beating ourselves up!

We look to tell people how to be and how to do things because we want a specific outcome, in a timely manner. As we look to control others, we become nag bags! This doesn't allow other people to be themselves and feel comfortable around us, creating conflict. In these times it is good to take a deep breath, get back into our Heartspace, use your S.E.X.Y. 5 Triggers™ or 00S.E.X.Y.™ and find ways to be flexible and fluid.

S.E.X.Y. Share

Let go of control! Swap it for going more with the flow!

TIME TO REFLECT

- How full is your emotional bank account? Fuelled or depleted?

- Define what self-love means to you?

- On a scale of 1-10 (10 being the highest) where would you score your self-worth?

- What's your 00S.E.X.Y.™?

- If money and time were limitless, what would you do for yourself?

ANY "AHA" MOMENTS?

Anything to bin and let go of?

_____

_____

_____

_____

_____

For a printable exercise sheet for you to work through, go to

M Club at www.mudrikademaria.com/MClub

I'm excited for your progress!

CHAPTER EIGHT

SLIP INTO YOUR S.E.X.Y. SELF OUTSIDE AND TURN HEADS

Let's get you on the catwalk of life! I use the analogy of catwalk because I love fashion. You don't see what goes on behind the scenes of a fashion show. The models come out looking perfect, oozing self-confidence, strutting their thing, and making it look effortless S.E.X.Y. All you see is the end result, you don't see the stressful, sometimes painful transformation that they have had to go through that day. Trust me, I know, I have worked behind the scenes of the Dior fashion show.

They will have had hours of having their hair pulled around and styled, layers of make-up put on, been pulled into corsets and most the time forcing themselves into shoes and clothes that are not made for comfort. Followed by absolute chaos to change from one outfit to the next.

In the same way that the models go through a journey to look and have the confidence to strut their S.E.X.Y. thing, you will have gone through a transformation reading this book, no matter how small. This has been a process to empower you and give you the confidence to walk the rest of your life runway ready.

The outside is not so important to everybody, however, in my opinion, women appreciate beautiful things and enjoy feeling good about themselves. When women look great on the outside, this makes us feel good, and when we feel good, we feel more empowered and confident! When women don't take care of themselves on the outside, I have found it to be because they need to work on their self-confidence, self-worth and self-love.

S.E.X.Y. Share
"Every day is a fashion show, and the world is the runway".
Well said Coco Chanel.

HOLD YOUR HEAD AND STANDARDS HIGH (AND YOUR HEELS)

Confident women should be studied and looked at as role models, they turn heads no matter what they are wearing, they take pride in themselves. I noticed so many confident, S.E.X.Y. and fashion-conscious women in France and Italy. I believe this stems from their upbringing, they are taught to have pride in the way they show up. Even in their everyday life, they walk the streets with grace and elegance with an air of fabulousness.

It all comes back to being the designer of your own life, strutting your own thing, your own catwalk for the rest of your life, whatever that looks like for you. Often, I will walk into the office with a pair of jeans and a T-shirt, but because I wear them with pride and confidence, I still feel the epitome of S.E.X.Y.

INSTANT S.E.X.Y. 4™

Here are four instant ways of being S.E.X.Y. on the outside. They don't cost a penny! Again, in no particular order:

1. Posture. Walk tall, shoulders back, head held high with grace. Suddenly you show confidence and have more of a presence.

2. Smile. A smile is one of the most beautiful things a woman can wear. People are drawn to and appreciate a smiling, happy person … it just makes you and others feel great.

3. Eye contact. Give people eye contact and connect with them. The eyes are the window to the soul. It is the ultimate connection.

4. Be yourself. If people don't connect with you, it's ok, millions of other people will.

There is a printable version available in the M Club at www.mudrikademaria.com/MClub

BODY IMAGE

There is a lot to say about body image. We have a lot of things we compare ourselves to, especially with social media right now. It is important to look at what insecurities came up for you in this book. We have to accept ourselves for who we are. If there are things you want to change about your body, you can do, but do it from a place of kindness. If you feel you need to improve anything, focus on moving forward, from a place of acceptance and love.

You will see pictures of me on Instagram. I am not a size zero. Do I want to lose a couple pounds here and there? Yes, always, because I love food and eating out! But when I look in the mirror, I accept and love myself for who I am in that moment!

HEALTH AND NUTRITION

Exercise can be overwhelming and intimidating. Often, we get stuck wondering what exercise to do and we try to copy other people. Connecting to who you are and coming from that space to find out what you enjoy doing is a game changer! I used to go to the gym, which I really didn't enjoy, but connecting to my true self, I found walking in nature was my thing and I love it! This a triple whammy for me because I am getting exercise and at the same time connecting to my senses, Mother Nature, and my FeM Essence™. I equally enjoy dancing, which is another way I can get fit, and it allows me to socialise at the same time.

Nutrition is also super important. When I was feeling unS.E.X.Y., I wasn't eating well because I didn't prioritise myself. Nutrition is absolutely key to living a S.E.X.Y. life. When we are healthy, we have the energy to do whatever we desire! And we get the side effect of looking radiant and hot!

Where do we find that balance between the food that we love and the food that is full of nutrition? It's about getting creative! A lot of healthy food can be bland and makes people feel unsatisfied. I have found the secret is to use seasoning and have an open mind to new foods and different cuisines. You will be surprised at how many healthy options there are out there, that taste great. It's tempting to look for the next best food plan and go on loads of yo diets, but the best thing is making nutrition part of your lifestyle.

A quick example for you: I always added seasoning to vegetables, even if it was only garlic, salt and pepper and as a result my kids love vegetables so much we have to serve them at the end of the meal because otherwise, they would eat them first and not eat their main meal!

Being fit and doing some form of exercise makes you feel good about yourself; it helps you connect to your body more and it raises your energy field and aura. People who look after themselves have a high level of self-love and self-worth.

BEAUTY AND HAIR

I used to be a beauty therapist many years ago, and it was something I loved to do. Keeping your beauty regime simple is key. We can sometimes overcomplicate it with sixteen products to do in the morning and the evening, etc.

Yes, all of these things are brilliant, and they really do work, but we live in the real world, and life does get in the way. The top three products you really need are a cleanser, toner, and moisturiser, and they do the job absolutely perfectly. When you get into that daily habit, feel free to add other products into your regime, but get that habit nailed first!

Get your "Defluff" on! One of the most feminine and sexiest things is having soft, silky, hairless skin, and it's so simple to do. We can sometimes overcomplicate it because we wait to make an appointment at the salon and sometimes, we simply just don't have the time. Don't use this as an excuse, there are so many products you can buy to do this at home, for yourself.

S.E.X.Y. Share

Just because the world isn't watching,
doesn't mean you can't still look good for you.

Who agrees that when your hair looks great, you feel great! Hair is my number one thing to express my S.E.X.Y. Self outside, so having my hair blow-dried is a must to for me and always makes me feel amazing. I have it done once a week without fail. Even my friends will comment and say, "Nice blow-job", oops, I meant blow-dry!

There have been times where I have not been able to get my hair blow-dried, so I have made it a priority for me to do it myself. Despite it taking over an hour to do, it's non-negotiable for me. Now I am not saying that you need to spend that much time doing your hair, but at a minimum, a rough dry, serum, tongs, straightener or at least a brush, can easily transform your hair.

NAILS

We use our hands so much when we are talking to people, and they are seen a lot. I have my nails done with gel polish because it lasts for weeks. However, if you don't have the resources to do this invest in a light nude polish. Apply one coat. The beauty of this is that it gives a shine and when it chips off, it doesn't show, making it low maintenance. As for your feet, if you can't get into a salon to get a Pedi, a few coats of dark polish will work a dream.

MAKE-UP

Having been a qualified make-up artist, I was taught that make-up is always about enhancing your natural beauty. It is about looking at your features and enhancing them, not completely changing them! There is a big trend of contouring make-up, which I don't fully agree with for day by day, as this changes your natural features, instead of enhancing them. If you're using contouring make-up for a photo shoot, then I get it.

If you want to do a full face of make-up and you've got the time – amazing. However, if you don't, and you've got a busy lifestyle or you don't really know how to put on your make-up very well, go for some simple things, such as a tinted moisturiser. It's very light, making it easy to apply. A touch of concealer under the eyes and on any unwanted blemishes is a brilliant alternative to foundation.

You don't have to wear eyeshadow all the time, a simple eyeliner and brush of mascara will just open up your sparkling eyes. To finish it off, a hint of lipstick and sass.

S.E.X.Y. Social Share

A touch of lip gloss will give you luscious,

sexy irresistible lips.

Go on, put some on now,

take a pic and share!

UNLEASH YOUR S.E.X.Y. FASHIONISTA

You may like to go out in a pair of joggers, a t-shirt and still feel confident and S.E.X.Y. That is fine, but please make sure you are doing it for the right reasons, not to hide behind the frump.

For me, confidence on the outside is being chic and "fabulous", as my stylist Karen says! I take a huge amount of pride in how I show up on the outside. I love to look good, I am passionate about beauty and glamour. I like to pass by a mirror and see my reflection and think, damn you look good! Go girl! I sometimes wonder if this is because of my inbuilt Indian goddess because when you wear a saree, it is very feminine, flowing, colourful, bright and a little sexy with your midriff showing.

You don't have to follow the latest trend, invest in timeless pieces that you can re-wear for many years and mix and match to create different outfits. Don't save your favourite clothes for a special occasion, every day is a special occasion!

Showing up glamorous does not always mean spending loads of money, it is about paying attention to what you like and trying on different things. I sometimes wear a business outfit, head to toe, that cost me under £90, but people would never know it.

What is your signature look, what do you like? If you don't know, spend some time looking at some magazines and look for some inspiration. Follow some people on social media that will give you some ideas. But when putting a look together, keep it simple; a pair of jeans, white t-shirt, trainers or a pair of loafers, works a treat.

Lights, camera, action!

TIME TO REFLECT

- What do you keep for special occasions that you can wear more?

- What will you commit to doing for your S.E.X.Y. outside?

- If money and time were limitless, what would you do for yourself?

- Magic mirror moments – stand in front of a mirror, preferably full length. Look at yourself for a minimum of 1 minute, the longer the better. Look at parts of yourself and allow your thoughts to flow…come back to the book and write down what came up for you.

ANY "AHA" MOMENTS?

Anything to bin and let go of?

_____

_____

_____

_____

_____

For a printable exercise sheet for you to work through, go to

M Club at www.mudrikademaria.com/MClub

I'm excited for your progress!

Chapter Nine

Catwalk Your S.E.X.Y. Self on the Runway of Life

I hope you have enjoyed your Unleash Your S.E.X.Y. journey, learning what S.E.X.Y. means to you…letting go of some of your baggage, reconnecting to your S.E.X.Y. Self, connecting to your heart, body, soul and intuition, balancing your FeM Essence™, powering up your S.E.X.Y. Self and slipping into your S.E.X.Y. Self outside. There has been a lot that we have covered, and even if you have only picked up a few little nuggets, this is a win. Celebrate!

It's time to D.R.E.S.S.-Up and become the designer of your life, this is going to take some "woo woo" and some "do do"!

D.	R.	E.	S.	S.	-	Up
r	i	n	E.	t		
e	t	v	X.	a		
a	u	i	Y.	n		
m	a	r		d		
s	l	o		a		
	s	n		r		
		m		d		
		e		s		
		n				
		t				

There is a printable version available in the M Club at www.mudrikademaria.com/MClub

DREAMS

Do you have dreams, goals and aspirations? Are they yours, as often we pick up other people's along the way? I would like to encourage you to review your dreams and create new ones if you so desire. Maybe you have even received some new insights and inspiration from reading this book.

- What are your dreams and aspirations?

- Who is the true S.E.X.Y. you? (Your S.E.X.Y. Self/Social/Sexual)

- What does your S.E.X.Y. Self inside look like?

- What does your S.E.X.Y. Self outside look like?

RITUALS

Rituals are often known as habits. I see rituals as actions that you do on a regular basis, and they move you closer to your dreams and filling up your emotional bank account. From the topics of the book, you will have learned ways to help you Unleash Your S.E.X.Y. Rituals are a form of self-care, to give you self-love and build your self-worth.

- What is your letting go ritual for when patterns show up in the future?

- What will you do to bring you joy and happiness?

- What will you do to use your S.E.X.Y. 6™ Senses (S.E.X.Y. 5 Triggers™)?

- How will you keep yourself in your FeM Essence™ balance?

- How will you fill up your emotional bank account (self-love, self-worth)?

- How will you commit to doing your 00S.E.X.Y.™?

- What will you do for your S.E.X.Y. outside?

S.E.X.Y. Share
Make space/time for yourself,
and make yourself a priority.

List all your rituals daily, weekly and monthly that make you feel your S.E.X.Y. Self. You can see a list of mine on the

M Club (www.mudrikademaria.com/MClub)

S.E.X.Y. Share
Get yourself organised by creating lists, buying a journal, subscribing to that membership, joining the gym, booking that treatment...more examples are on the M Club at www.mudrikademaria.com/MClub.

ENVIRONMENT

Your environment is very important. This is mainly people you surround yourself with, but also, your space and the things around you. You may need to declutter the people in your life. I am a big believer in who you surround yourself with is who you become.

Detox your life of people who do not support you. You don't need to totally cut them out, simply choose to spend less time with them. Some friends will not understand you unleashing your S.E.X.Y. Don't allow them to project their own insecurities onto you. My girlfriends are like an epic box of chocolates; they all have different personalities and remind me of all the things I can be in life. Be around women who empower you and inspire you to be your best self.

They want to keep you the same because that is what they are used to. Look to find a community of like-minded people and women who are supportive and looking to unleash their S.E.X.Y. That is why I created the free membership site and a closed Facebook group, so we can be a part of a supportive community where we can empower each other and share tips and tools.

Create a space in your home, just as men have man caves... I believe every woman should have a haven. Mine is in the living room, where I have music, candles, and dimmed lights.

- Do you have a supportive environment?

- What changes do you need to make to your current environment?

- List people in your life who are negative.

- List people in your life who are positive.

- We can be really bad at asking for help because we don't want to appear vulnerable. Who do you have in your life that you can ask for help from?

- Join my M Club to build that supportive community around you at www.mudrikademaria.com/MClub.

S.E.X.Y.

SELF-CONFIDENT

- What is self-confidence for you?

- What will you do more of to build your self-confidence?

- What will you say, "NO" to?

S.E.X.Y. Share

Sign up to M Club for free now and create your new S.E.X.Y. environment at www.mudrikademaria.com/MClub

---

EMPOWERED

- What empowers you? Create a list.

- Practising gratitude and appreciation helps us stay in the moment and enjoy what we have achieved and what we already have in our life. What do you appreciate in your life? What are you most grateful for?

XTREMELY YOU

- What did you learn about yourself?

- What do you remember about the little girl inside?

- What is your inner magic?

STANDARDS

Time to raise your S.E.X.Y. standards!

- Keep your self-talk in check. The first step to working on self-talk is awareness when you are aware, you can catch it trying to sabotage you. You can ask it to, "F**K off", kindly.

- Free yourself from "can't" – look to find a way where you can.

- I'm too busy – we get stuck in busy habits we don't even need to still be doing. Look at what is making you busy. Is it necessary?

- Turn your, "I should" into, "What if I could?"

- Don't play the victim – you are in charge of your own life – make the change.

- Don't compare yourself to others unless you are using them as inspiration to move forward.

- Keep your promises to yourself – this makes you a priority and builds your self-worth and self-love.

- Start today – progress is always good even if small and don't put things off.

- Focus on solutions – ask yourself good questions to find the solutions.

- Celebrate all your wins, no matter how small and fill up your emotional bank account.

- What Standards, from the above, will you now take on board (feel free to add some of your own)?

S.E.X.Y. Share

get a list of all your S.E.X.Y. standards for you to download/print of the M Club at www.mudrikademaria.com/MClub!
Stick It up somewhere to remind you of them.

Enjoy the dressing-up process, change is hard, however, with the focus of making you a priority and having a supportive community, it is time to DRESS UP and LEVEL UP your S.E.X.Y. SELF and LIFE.

CHAPTER TEN

TURN ON THE S.E.X.Y. WOW!

In order to achieve love, happiness, and success in your life, it takes 80% S.E.X.Y. Mindset and 20% skill. For example, you could get a stylist, to bring the 20% skill, and they can give you a makeover, however, if you are not feeling S.E.X.Y. on the inside, you will still feel shy, awkward and uncomfortable. It is likely that because of this, you will retreat back to your old wardrobe, and until you sort out your S.E.X.Y. Mindset, no change will be sustainable.

The philosophy I have been teaching you in this book has been to build your S.E.X.Y. Mindset. Can you imagine how much easier it will now be to go through life this way? You can use these philosophies in the wheel of life. The wheel of life covers all areas of your life, including health, relationships, financial wealth, career, family, spirituality, growth, charity, etc.

WHEEL OF LIFE

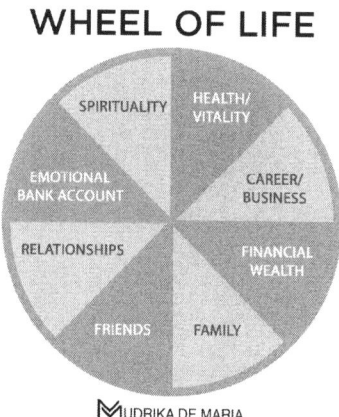

MUDRIKA DE MARIA

You are on the path of levelling up your S.E.X.Y. Mindset. You can use your S.E.X.Y. Self to attract amazing relationships, health, and financial wealth into your life. I have used these principles in my life and believe it is the most important thing you can do; to work on your S.E.X.Y. Self first, and everything else just flows into place.

S.E.X.Y. Share
If a woman builds her own pedestal,

she can't be knocked off.

WOW WOMEN OWNING WEALTH™

This brings me to my next philosophy which is, WOW! Women Owning Wealth. My definition of wealth is emotional wealth, financial wealth, and health. When these come together, you have certainty, freedom and bliss. I call this the Trilogy of Wealth, and when everything comes together, you have a wealthy life.

WOW!

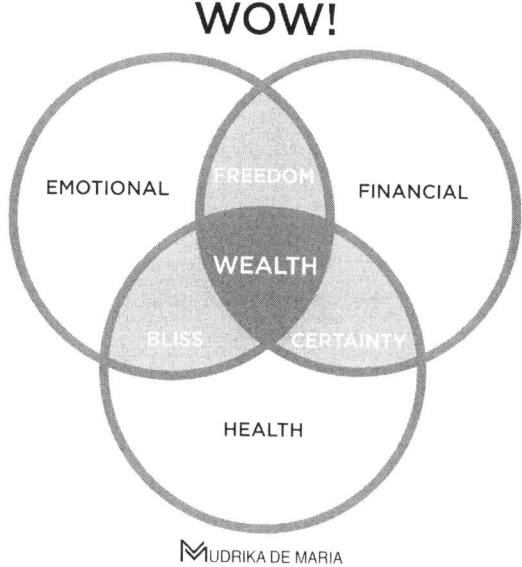

MUDRIKA DE MARIA

Emotional wealth is the S.E.X.Y. Mindset philosophy. Health, we touched on briefly in chapter 8. So now I come to the completion of the trilogy, financial wealth, which is another area in the wheel of life.

We could have been taught patterns, handed down through generations, that men are the providers. However, in the modern evolving world, we now have the opportunities to create our own financial wealth, and this allows us the freedom to do and have the things we desire.

I have always been passionate about creating my own financial wealth because I like the finer things in life, luxury (LUX). I love glamour, fashion, travelling, having experiences. For me, it is important to have the freedom and the ability to give back. I don't need material things to make me happy or feel loved. I feel loved and happy with the simplest things in life, such as words of affirmation and physical touch – a hug or a kiss. The LUX is just the cherry on the top.

In the Time to Reflect sections of this book, I ask the question, "If money and time were limitless, what would you do for yourself?" I am sure that you came up with many more things that you would do. Most people feel they can't do certain things because they don't focus on the fact that they could make money and time available by becoming financially independent.

I feel by being financially independent, it allows us to have a better quality of life, without being reliant on anybody else. This can show up in giving us freedom by allowing us to create time and have the resources to be able to afford to make ourselves a priority. How amazing would it be if you could afford to fulfil all your dreams and self-care needs? Such as affording a cleaner, a personal trainer, a mentor, nutritional meals, hair and beauty treatments, clothes. The list is endless.

I am grateful that my financial independence has allowed me to give back because I have more time and resources. Within Investment Mastery, we have a charitable branch to give back to the world and empower others, which is very fulfilling. IM Creating Ripples is about leaving ripples of positive change for long after we are gone, leaving a legacy. What would you do if you had financial independence or even freedom?

Often women will create financial wealth in masculine energy. This is because they feel they live in a man's world, and that's the only way. This is a sure way to lose your S.E.X.Y. Using the philosophy of Unleash Your S.E.X.Y., you can achieve wealth in your natural feminine flow, be that creative entrepreneur, investor or bossbabe, the world is your oyster.

IMPORTANCE OF HAVING A MENTOR

Having a mentor and being part of an empowering community is the key to your continued momentum. I have had mentors for over twenty years now, and I owe my success to being held accountable and inspired. It has been the best investment I have ever made – an investment in myself to be the best version of me and I wish that for all of you out there, to be living as your S.E.X.Y. Self. If you want to continue being a part of my S.E.X.Y. community, go to my M Club today (www.mudrikademaria.com/MClub).

IF I CAN DO IT, SO CAN YOU!

Anything is possible if you believe in yourself and stay true to your dreams by trusting the Universe. Even though it seemed like all the odds were against me, such as: overcoming my strong cultural patterns, lack of education, sudden loss of my mum, struggling to climb the corporate ladder, failed marriages, miscarriages, struggling with mummy guilt and constantly putting everyone else first, I still found a way to live the life that I wanted. I am just a normal person and if I can do it, so can you!

My wish for this book is for it to be an example for women who are looking to better their lives. There is nothing more rewarding and empowering than helping a fellow gal. Let's empower each other and bring people into our community by sharing our stories on social media. The good, the bad and the ugly. Let's be kind to each other, smile at a stranger, open a door for someone and give someone a compliment to make their day.

I made the mistake of thinking I'll be happy when I get there, when I achieve that "next dream." I missed out on living in the moment and being grateful for what I had in my life. Life is a journey, not a destination, and we should be enjoying it along the way. Stay true to who you are, you are perfect being irresistibly you.

Enjoy your S.E.X.Y.

Connect with me at:

Instagram: www.instagram.com/mudrikademaria

Facebook: www.facebook.com/groups/mudrikademaria

YouTube: www.youtube.com/mudrikademaria

Website: www.mudrikademaria.com

M Club: www.mudrikademaria.com/MClub

Printed in Poland
by Amazon Fulfillment
Poland Sp. z o.o., Wrocław

88245768R00081